June Lee was born in Suncheon, South Korea, and grew up in the countryside, playing and running around mountains and green fields. His childhood background instilled in him a love for adventure and nature. Even after the bike journey, he remains passionate about protecting the environment.

Moreover, he continuously strives to give back and provide significant help to others.

June Lee

THE ROAD TO ANFIELD

AUSTIN MACAULEY PUBLISHERS™
LONDON • CAMBRIDGE • NEW YORK • SHARJAH

Copyright © June Lee 2024

The right of June Lee to be identified as author of this work has been asserted by the author in accordance with sections 77 and 78 of the Copyright, Designs, and Patents Act 1988.

All rights reserved. No part of this publication may be reproduced, stored in a retrieval system, or transmitted in any form or by any means, electronic, mechanical, photocopying, recording, or otherwise, without the prior permission of the publishers.

Any person who commits any unauthorised act in relation to this publication may be liable for criminal prosecution and civil claims for damages.

All of the events in this memoir are true to the best of author's memory. The views expressed in this memoir are solely those of the author.

A CIP catalogue record for this title is available from the British Library.

ISBN 9781035801459 (Paperback)
ISBN 9781035801466 (ePub e-book)

www.austinmacauley.co.uk

First Published 2024
Austin Macauley Publishers Ltd®
1 Canada Square
Canary Wharf
London
E14 5AA

Prologue

Going to Liverpool Riding a Bicycle

When I first told them I had come up with a plan to ride a bicycle leaving for Liverpool and to learn football, they gave me advice like this:

"You should' rather go to Southeast Asia and enjoy some time there. And then fly by airplane with the same money. Doing that sounds insane."

They reacted like it's an absurd, sceptical, and outrageous plan.

However, when I think about it that kind of reaction gave me some energy for the challenge; to traverse the continent by bicycle.

Anyway, I think that if they had given me a positive response or an encouraging message, I could not have even started my journey.

It's like if people around you say, "You can't do this. Stop and try other things" and respond in negative way, then you can feel an obstinate feeling with some determination, thinking "I am gonna make this out to show off before you."

And I did so I finally made it.

It didn't take a lot of time to prepare the journey.

To accumulate some power to endure the long trip, I worked out lightly; like free gymnastics (without exercising tools) and, commuted by bicycle to get used to sitting on the chair.

If there was too much rain to get on the bicycle, I took the subway. When the weather was so good that I wanted to run out, then I ran. Except for these things, I substituted my training for riding a bicycle.

I figured out after finishing my trip, that people who travelled across the Eurasian continent with a motorbike or car, had met other people who already had the same experiences in order to get information and prepare for their trips.

But I met only one, whose name was "Hwang in Beom".

When I was finishing the bicycle trip and met him again, he said, "When I first met you first, I thought that you just had a plan."

He did not expect me to go because I did not seem like the kind of person who is ready for that trip.

The reason why I met him was to get to know how to get a sponsor.

I was worried about the future; what if there was no more money left for the trip, or if I spent all the money that I had saved in my life.

He said to me, "This trip is about putting aside all of your worries, concerns and calculations about the future So just leave when you're excited about it."

As I heard what he said, I just zoned out.

"I've been different. I decided to do something that I have dreamed about my entire life, but I have been worried too much, like I had lost the point of the tour.

After that, I stopped worrying about money and other things and just focused on travelling.

And I thought about a plan to share my trip with my friends.

For example, taking some pictures, writing postcards, and sending them to my friends in Korea. That is all of my preparation for the trip.

Just challenging without a plan.

When you went to university, I just put on the bicycle without any sign.

The Beginning of The Crossing of Eurasia: China

Road to Beijing

I had good luck from the beginning.

The fortune was brought by a Chinese friend, Brios, whom I met in the ship going to Tianjin.

I just started to talk to him, thinking if I communicated with him, I could get some information about China.

We got to know each other on the ship, and Brios invited me to a meeting with his friends, who had come to welcome Brios and his girlfriend, who were returning to Tianjin. including his girlfriend.

It was a party to welcome Brios returning from his Korea trip to Korea.

He was about to return to China after finishing his riding trip. For which he spent one week in Jeju Island, and another one week in Seoul.

Of course, I was an unexpected guest, but they sincerely welcomed me.

Travelling in an unfamiliar foreign country, interacting with local people, experiencing new cultures and being welcomed was so special for me, and it felt like being blessed at the start of a long trip.

Next day, after I left Brios, my real trip started—the lonely road that I should find.

People feel really lonely when they get in a situation where a person cannot expect another's help, and has to decide all by oneself.

The Chinese didn't understand English, and I didn't know Chinese characters. I didn't even understand the signs, so which sky should I look at and follow? I tried to find a sign that said "Beijing" but I couldn't find the Chinese letters. I just depended on a doubtful and basic iPhone map and kept pedalling.

Differing with the map, the road did not exist because its construction wasn't finished. Thankfully, some workers who worked on the spot helped me to find the paved road.

I could not understand anything they told me, but people have hands and feet that communicate. And somehow, I found out the way to Beijing, which meant I turned the first corner.

There are two main roads from Tianjin to Beijing.

I chose the road that Brios recommended to me, and soon, I got to know why.

It was so amazing to ride a bicycle on two-lane roads, lined with trees on both sides. I felt relaxed and the wind was refreshing.

There was one thing that was getting more and more on the road to Beijing. That was the CCTV.

There are a lot of CCTV cameras installed on roads in Korea as well, so you might be wondering 'what the problem is?'

But the CCTV cameras installed on the roads in Beijing are not like speeding or traffic enforcement cameras.

They are for monitoring the people who enter Beijing.

How did I know that? If you see that the camera moves in the direction that people are moving in, you can catch that it's a surveillance camera.

As I saw the cameras, I felt like I was being monitored because I was, inclined to think that, and it made me feel very unpleasant and disgusting.

What I felt was even more unfamiliar, was that to enter Beijing, we had to go through a checkpoint, like when crossing a border before entering. Isn't that weird?

Obviously, I had already been thoroughly checked in from Tianjin, and I was just trying to go into Beijing but, I had to go through security again.

It wasn't just for me, a foreigner.

All trucks and cars entering Beijing must go through checkpoints. We cannot imagine this situation in Korea.

After I experienced this kind of situation, I thought Korea had more liberty and how much Beijing cares for security.

As good luck would have it, it started raining the day I entered Beijing.

For the period of time I stayed in Beijing, it rained every day so I had to stay in, and spent almost all the time at a hostel.

It could have turned into a boring time for me, but luckily I had friends; Florian and Robert from Germany.

I had nothing to do, so we watched the Euro Cup group stages together and became friends easily. Just like the saying, that in order to get close, you have to have the same hobbies, people who like football seem to get along quickly.

It's something we can't know in detail from a short-term relationship, but I liked them, and we got closer.

I did not travel that many times, but could feel that a travelling experience makes people spill out their stories like magic.

Maybe it's because people don't calculate their profit while sharing travelling experiences. Anyway, they asked me to contact them when I got to Germany so they could invite me.

When I stayed in Beijing, I was able to meet Brios again.

Because I had gotten his phone number before we broke up in Tianjin.

He invited me to lunch, and said it was a very famous restaurant, I can't remember the exact name of.

People who didn't make a reservation were waiting in line, so it must have been a famous restaurant.

Brios said that Beijing noodle named 'jajangmyeon' is a more traditional Beijing dish than Peking Duck, so he ordered Beijing jajangmyeon and various unknown traditional dishes, even a Chinese rice cake for dessert.

When I saw the BMW SUV driven by his girlfriend who was coming to Tianjin, I thought, 'People who are living in China must have these kinds of cars'.

But that day when I met them again, they took another car, a Mercedes Benz, and I realised he was quite wealthy.

Anyway, we just got acquainted and talked on the ship from Korea, but I was touched to see him treating me as a guest, and cherishing such a relationship.

I could experience the Chinese culture of cherishing guests by meeting him. Since Brios' surname is King, I called him Mr. King.

The image that comes to mind when we hear the words 'Mr. King' (Wang Seobang) was, the king of the silk troupe who has wealth and a feeling of intimacy. I smiled by myself because Brios' appearance was just like that!

Riding on the Great Wall

The day I left Beijing, the weather was absolutely perfect!
Everyone says it's really hard to see a blue sky in Beijing, but it was that blue sky. Maybe it was because it had been raining for a few days.
I took a picture with the precious 'blue sky' and Tiananmen in the background.

Tiananmen Square was full of soldiers because German Chancellor, Merkel, was visiting China. It wasn't very peaceful.

It's hard to imagine Gwanghwamun Square with soldiers gathering with their guns in Korea. Oh, while I was taking pictures before Tiananmen that day, something happened.

At the beginning of the trip, I prepared two Korean flags, Taegeukgi, and put one of them on my bicycle. But after taking some pictures, I noticed that the Taegeukgi was gone.

I tried to find it, but I couldn't.

Could it be that the soldiers who passed by pulled it out? It was absurd and while it made me feel angry, on the other hand, I also felt terrified.

It seemed that the soldier hated to see me roaming freely with the Taegeukgi on my bicycle, for their viewpoint in a communist country.

I thought I should not lose the remaining Taegeukgi so I decided to keep it from my bicycle in China.

Passing through the Olympic Stadium, I pedalled towards the Great Wall, which I wanted to visit the most in China.

The Great Wall is around 70 kilometres from downtown Beijing.

It is not too hard to find the way. Just follow the signs of 'The Great Wall' and pedal in that direction. It is an easy road to pedal just 50 kilometres from Beijing.

While enjoying it so easily without any effort, but I suddenly met high mountains and the Great Wall of China looming along the mountain ridge.

The moment I saw the Great Wall suddenly appearing in front of me, I couldn't believe what I saw. I didn't have anything else to say. It was truly an amazing sight.

If you plan to go to the Great Wall, I would recommend you to rent a motorcycle from downtown Beijing. That way you can move a lot more freely than on a group tour; you are not by time, and most importantly, the feeling of seeing the Great Wall for the first time! You will understand how I felt, when you see the Great Wall appearing as you turn the last corner.

Now it was an uphill climb.

If I had a motorcycle, I could climb the Great Wall without any problem; just admiring and reflecting on the amazing views, but I chose to ride a bicycle so, I had to pedal up the hill.

Was it halfway up?

Without my intention, a curse came out of my mouth. And it was mumbled like this: "Such a crazy Chinese…How did they make this high wall? I look up to you guys…'"

I felt a sharp pain in my thighs like they would burst.

It lasted a few hours, and we finally managed to reach the bottom of the Chang Cheng Great Wall.

From this place, people should take a cable car up to the top of the mountain; seeing the Great Wall from the top of the castle is a different feeling—it. seems like a dignified dragon is roaming the ridge.

I imagined the people who built this castle a long time ago, burned bricks and carried them while climbing the mountain.

I really want to recommend you to visit it.

If you have a chance to go to the Great Wall, I would recommend you to rent a motorcycle from the downtown of Beijing for one day.

I don't know how we can rent a motorcycle but renting it would be easy. I saw lots of people who rode Chinese motorcycles.

A Woman I Met in Datong

When I planned my bicycle trip, I decided to visit three places, which are; Lake Baikal, St. Petersburg, three Baltic countries, Germany, and the final target city, Liverpool.

The rest of the travelling destinations were randomly planned; to be recommended by locals or travellers I met along the way, so I didn't have any special destinations in mind.

Besides, I thought no planned travelling could be better than getting along with the local people I met.

In short, I wanted to meet local people to communicate, and to get some information or recommendations about nice restaurants, and hidden, fancy tour attractions.

Datong is the place I got to know about in this way.

It was not recommended by locals, but by German friends I met in Beijing Hostel.

They did not visit the place but got recommended by other people to visit this wonderful city. After they made me aware of Datong, I searched the map and found that I needed to go back a bit, but decided to stop by.

Of course, even then, I had no idea why Datong was famous and recommended. The way to Datong is the worst I have ever seen.

There are a lot of mountains and trucks in the north of China.

I saw more trucks on the way to Datong than the trucks I have seen while living in Korea for 25 years.

After arriving in Datong, I got to know that it is a region where a lot of coal is produced, so many trucks transport coal.

Anyway, I should've brought a mask because I inhaled soot and coal dust on the road. During the journey to Datong, I was worried about my lungs.

I was riding a bike every day to exercise, but on the way to Datong, I felt that my lungs were getting worse and worse, and I felt like I was ruining my body, rather than getting healthy by riding the bike.

I could not understand Chinese drivers.

Whether it's a tight road, a two-lane road or a four-lane road, it doesn't matter; once they see space, they overtake other cars.

Imagine how Chinese drivers overtake on a tight round-way four-lane road!

When both up-way lanes are blocked, Chinese drivers check the shoulder and, if there is room, they attack that side first.

Then, if they can no longer drive on the shoulder, they will boldly enter the downbound lane and overtake the downbound road.

Don't you think it's really unbelievable? How do they drive like that? Besides, when someone enters the downbound lane and drives on the lane, the others follow behind him like biting his tails one by one.

And then, it makes the situation worse because the downbound lane also gets jammed.

What's more unbelievable is that I've never seen any traffic accident while they drove like that.

When I arrived in Datong, I got a hostel and headed to Yungang Grottoes, the nearest tourist attraction in downtown Datong.

When I entered Datong, it wasn't so hot, but it got hotter moving from the downtown of Datong to Yungang Grottoes.

The cracks on the road were roughly filled with tar and it was so hot that the tar melted from the heat and stuck to my bike tires, making the bike slower and slower, and blowing in the headwinds that drove me crazy.

It took about 20 kilometres from the downtown of Datong to reach Yungang Grottoes, but it felt much farther away than that.

I even thought about going back to Datong halfway through. But after many twists and turns, I arrived at Yungang Grottoes. I tried to remove the tar from the tires, but it was very difficult to remove; the tar was stuck.

Luckily, however, I met a good friend at the Yungang Grottoes. Her name is Fan.

She was bowing to the largest Buddha in Yungang Grottoes.

She asked me to take pictures of her bowing to the Buddha, and after that we talked naturally.

She was studying in the Graduate School of Architecture in New York, and said that she visited Yungang Grottoes every summer to look around traditional buildings in China, could say "'Thank you'" in Korean and had a plan to visit Korea next month.

Though I am not good at speaking English, I was so happy to meet someone to communicate with after a long time.

I asked her to go out with me and have dinner together, and she was willing to allow it!

She was not from Datong, but she knew many things about this city since she had visited it many times.

We visited a restaurant for dinner whose dumplings are famous. What was more impressive and delicious than the main dish, (dumplings), was a dish made with sliced cucumbers and a special sauce. It was like eating cucumber noodles. Really unpredictable flavour.

I don't know the exact name but if I have the chance to visit again, I would try cucumber noodles again!

I think it might be a nice food for the summer season.

The next day, I looked around famous tour attractions near Datong, with the taxi driver offered by the hostel.

The best among them was the temple built on a cliff. It was called 'Hyeongongsa'.

Looking at the pictures, you might think that it is familiar like visiting that spot, but you would think that the old Chinese people were really amazing.

Long time ago, everything was calculated mathematically and architecturally, and to build a temple that can be maintained until now, without any machines.

I used to hear that China was the most prosperous country in the world before the end of the Qing Dynasty, but I really thought that was not wrong after seeing this view.

Tomorrow, I leave Datong, where China's character is really strong. Datong had lots of things to eat and see.

I felt the majesty of Datong Castle that has stood for hundreds of years.

Datong would be a more memorable city because of meeting Fan, who left pleasant memories.

Towards the Border of Mongolia

I left Datong and pedalled toward Inner Mongolia, and soon I reached the border.

It took about 400 kilometres from Datong to the border, and it felt like the desert started from Inner Mongolia.

There were only a few cities in sight, and beyond those few cities, it was just a green meadow. There was really nothing but green meadows.

No hills, only a few cars to pass.

There was just a two-lane road that was not in a good condition.

There were so many wild horses in Inner Mongolia.

They roamed around in groups, and when it was hot, they went under a tree or in a large sewer to escape the heat, and then moved somewhere in the afternoon.

It was late in the evening when I was setting up my tent on the meadow and getting ready to spend the night.

A herd of horses appeared, from where I did not know, and rushed. In this situation, I suddenly had a terrible thought.

What if the horses did not notice my tent and trample on it at midnight? Just to be safe, I laid down on my bike in front of my ten thinking that my bike would be ruined but my life would be saved.

The nights in Inner Mongolia are really cold.

In the daytime, the heat is over 30 degrees, but when the sun goes down, the temperatures drop to under 10 degrees.

Besides, to lose my load, I brought a very thin and light sleeping bag that had been in my house, so I planned to suffer this cold.

After setting up the tent, I would fall asleep in an instant because of the fatigue accumulated by pedalling all day, but woke up in the middle of the night from the cold.

It used to repeat; to wake up from the cold and go back to sleep.

Finally, as soon as I arrived in the last Chinese city, Erenhot, I headed to the market and I bought a very thick, and good sleeping back which looked like it could stand cold, no matter how much it was. I consoled myself that I would no longer be shivering from the cold.

While rearranging my body and mind at a hotel, I searched about Mongolia, where I would be going the next day.

And then, it dawned on me that I had to venture into the heart of the Gobi Desert. While I was aware of the existence of the Gobi Desert in Mongolia, I had never truly considered that I would be traversing its vast expanse. The realization hit me like a wave, and I found myself grappling with the idea.

The cost of accommodation was high, but I felt that I must stay one more day to get information, and searched on cafés and blogs on the Internet, but that drove me into more fear.

Those who had travelled the Gobi Desert before me wrote that it was a dirt road, and that travellers should check all the small towns and markets, and prepare a small, 500-millilitre bottle of water in case the water ran out.

The information was so meaningful for me, but I felt anxiety, fear, and worry, instead of thinking that I am lucky I got to know about this information.

But just worrying could not solve any problem. And I had done nothing but worry in my life.

First of all, I enjoyed a last supper with the traditional Chinese food that I had loved while riding a bicycle from China. And then, hypnotised myself that everything would be perfect and fell asleep.

Tips Bike Tour in China

Making a Visa

Korean passports are very convenient. With just the passport, you can travel to almost any country without a visa. But China, a very close country, is an exception.

When I tried to apply for a visa before starting my riding trip, I found out that Chinese visa is divided into short-term, mid-long-term, and long term visas, depending on the staying period.

I applied for a 60-day, mid to long-term visa.

Communication in the Disconnected World

What Brios told me on the ship heading to Tianjin was that all social media platforms such as Google, Facebook, and Instagram are blocked in China.

What I got to know after arriving in China is, that not just SNSs like above, but also the most famous application in Korea, named KakaoTalk, sometimes doesn't work as well.

Internet users can only use sites that are in Chinese.

You cannot use a text translator on Google, so you have to know basic Chinese words before leaving.

Accommodation for Chinese Only

Chinese accommodations are divided in two; a place where that only Chinese can stay, and a place where both Chinese and foreigners can stay.

The latter one for both Chinese and foreigners is uploaded on the hotel reservation applications. The biggest difference between the two accommodations is the price. Accommodations that are only available for Chinese are really cheap.

I entered a hotel showing the sign 'Hotel' in Chinese, without this information, I could not stay because I was not Chinese, several times, and could stay just this once luckily.

Thick sleeping bag.

I thought that it must be summer when I would pass Siberia, so I prepared a shabby sleeping bag that I had not used for a long time.

Before I entered Inner Mongolia, I was able to sleep and endure the night without severe discomfort with a thin sleeping bag, but after entering Inner Mongolia, I suffered a lot from the cold.

Since the temperature difference between days and nights is severe in Inner Mongolia, I really recommend that you should prepare a thick sleeping bag in advance, or purchase one before.

Bicycle Mask

Driving on the road can be painful because of soot and dust generated by cars passing by.

Particularly, on the way to Datong, there were lot of trucks carrying coal, so when I passed the road, I turned into a panda because everything on my face was black except for the area around the eyes, where I was wearing sunglasses.

In order to protect your lungs, you should take a bicycle mask.

Mongolia, the Great Mother Nature

Crisis, and a Good Start

I thought of entering the Gobi Desert immediately after crossing the Mongolian border, but an unexpected good relationship was made in Zamiin-Uud, the beginning of my trip to Mongolia, so I stayed there for a few days.

First, I'll explain the process of crossing the border of China. You must get in the car to cross the border. On my way out of downtown Erenhot and into Mongolia, jeeps started haggling with me. I felt like I was take the blame for it if I hastily ended the bargain with them and took the jeep. You know, that's how people feel. So it's like you often buy things all the way inside because it's going to be expensive if you go to the market and buy it early at the entrance. Anyway, I thought I should go near the border and bargain again. So I thought there would probably be more cars, and so I could choose a cheaper car according to the law of supply and demand. But wow, lucky me, the day I crossed the border was the opposite, whether it was a day when there was not much luggage going into Mongolia from China. So even though I wasted two hours, I managed to get a jeep at a higher price than what I saw on the blog the day before. There were luggage going into Mongolia, my bicycle, a Mongolian returning home, me, and the Mongolian owner of the jeep.

The Mongolian and I walked into the border office, and the jeep and its owner went separately to the vehicle inspection spot. There was no problem. The Mongolian who was accompanying me waited for the jeep to pass after completing the Chinese immigration and Mongolia immigration. After about two hours I waited for it? The jeep with my bicycle wouldn't come out of the checkpoint. I wondered if the Mongolian who came in the jeep with me had a strange idea, and he approached another car owner who got out after the inspection and asked him about the situation. Oh my god! It was that the owner of the jeep we rode together didn't bring his passport and went back to China. I thought the world was coming to an end.

"Oh, what should I do, how can I find my bicycle?"

I went back to the checkpoint and asked the staff how to find my bicycle, but to nothing was available. I couldn't speak a word in Mongolian, so I tried to explain it in body language in all sorts of ways, but it wasn't enough to make them understand. Of course they might not have been interested in my situation at all.

What was fortunate was that there was the Mongolian who accompanied me. He was also in the same situation as me when he crossed the checkpoint with a huge load in the trunk behind the jeep. So I thought he was the only one I could trust. Because he could speak the same language. I tagged after him wherever he went. Things started to change a little in the nervous time, which was that an English-speaking staff arrived at work.

When I explained the whole story, he reassured me to find out what was going on. Ah, something was about to get worked out, and the Mongolian who accompanied me shouted at me.

"Bicycle, here, here!"

Can you guess roughly? Yes! My bicycle had been at the checkpoint in China all that time. I started to calm down thinking that I could find my bicycle. I almost cried when I saw my Mongolian fellow going back to the checkpoint in China and dragging his luggage and my bicycle. Not to mention that I almost lost my bicycle, which was only a few weeks old, all the luggage except my passport was in the jeep. It is that I was just starting my trip, I mean, I hadn't even start it properly, and it is that I was so sad that I almost had to get back to Korea. Again, it was a terrible moment. At the first time I heard that the jeep went back to China, I had one idea that came up to my mind. "I've been scammed." I was just absent-minded. A Korean country bumpkin who has to go back to Korea after being scammed by people who don't speak the same language. But justice was alive, and fate was in favour of me. The moment I saw my Mongolian companion dragging my bicycle from the checkpoint was perhaps the happiest moment ever! I didn't know how many thoughts and emotions raise and disappeared! They were moments that I can never forget.

When I picked up my bicycle and tried to leave the border, a Mongolian staff grabbed me and said, "You must take a car at the border," and he told me that he will call a vehicle that I can ride for free. And thanks to the staff, I was able to get on a car and get out of the border.

Once I crossed the border, I first entered Zamiin-Uud. Because I had to prepare first to ride to Gobi Desert the day after. There were only three hotels in Zamiin-Uud, but I went to the three places one by one, compared them, and got the cheapest room.

What was urgent was to repair the bicycle. It was because the screw that had fastened the carrier was missing. I had managed to get a hotel in Mongolia where I couldn't communicate, but how else should I explain that I had to tighten the missing screw?

I had no choice but to experience it. I dragged my bicycle in front of the owner of the hotel, pointed out where the screw is supposed to be in, pointed out where the screw was gone, and made all sorts of gestures like, "It's gone!" He didn't understand at first, but after a while he talked to his wife, he beckoned me to follow him. Just in case, I followed the owner of the hotel to the only hardware store in the neighbourhood with my bicycle. Shortly after the owner of the hotel said something, Dashka, who ran the hardware store, brought a container with various kinds of screws. And he looked at me. The eyes were talking like this.

"Which screw are you looking for?"

I sighed instead of answering. I thought I explained it for about 30 minutes at the hotel already... After a few seconds of silence, Dashka asked me.

"Can you speak English?"

Hallelujah! I gave Dashka an explanation, showing where the screw fell out. While looking for a matching screw, Dashka who asked me, "Where are you from?" and "How did you end up coming here?" asked me to come with him, saying that he likes to ride bicycles and that he has a friend who fixes bicycles. Saying that if I need anything for a bicycle, I can bring it. And he went to his friend's house with me where he repaired bicycles and brought a carrier and installed it at the front of my bicycle. It was the place where I was going to load my sleeping bag. That way, he thought that I could load other luggages on the rear carrier. So we naturally talked about football while spending hours together. football was a universal language as expected. The reason why I wanted to go to Liverpool by bicycle was to study football. "Wow, that's amazing. We're going to play football on the schoolyard tonight. Do you want to join us?"

If it's football, it's definitely OK! Thanks to him, I had a special experience of kicking balls at the school's artificial turf field at the entrance of the Gobi Desert. The four corners of the field were covered with sand, and we had to stop kicking balls in the sandstorm, but it was really fun. The Mongolian friends knew how to kick balls well. Not only my peers but also the students at that school kicked balls with us, and anyone who likes football will know. It's a bit awkward at first, but after playing a few games together, we become friends. It was the same with the Mongolian friends. After the game, everyone had become friends. It had been a long time since I kicked balls with such excitement. As if I was going to stay there with no plans to go to the Gobi Desert the day after.

Was football a lucky messenger? Dashka asked me when the game was over.

"We're going to play basketball. Do you want to join us?"

What? We had just kicked balls for three games. Basketball? I shook my head. "No, I'm fine. I'm too tired. And I have to ride my bicycle in the Gobi Desert tomorrow."

"Stay a little longer! Come to my house and stay a few more days tomorrow instead of staying at the hotel."

The moment I heard what Dashka's said, I thought like this. "Right, this is how a trip is to hang out like this." Then I nodded and accepted his favour.

I spent the night at the hotel and went to Dashka's house in the morning, and it felt like I was visiting an old friend's house. And with no prior plan, I ended up staying at Dashka's house for three more days. Dashka's friends always came to the store and watched TV or played cards together, ate meals prepared by Dashka's mother, played basketball in the evening, and rode bicycles. I got along with them too. Like friends I had known for a long time.

Once, Dashka told me that there was something he really wanted for me to try. It was the brain of a lamb!

"A lamb's brain?"

"Yes, the brain in the lamb's head!"

"Oh, thank you so much, but I don't think I can eat it…"

But he got in the car without listening to me, started the engine, picked up his friend Baija, and took me to a restaurant. I made a face that I never wanted to eat it, but they seemed to make sure to make me it at all costs. The restaurant wasn't ready to open yet, so we had to wait about 30 minutes, but the good news was that Dashka lacked patience. I thought that they'd just leave the restaurant and go back home, but this time they went to the butcher's. I couldn't believe the sight of the butcher shop with my eyes open. I was sure that the butcher's shops in Korea were nothing compared to here. The cows were hung with their whole bodies peeled off, and I think I saw all the organs that were not seen in Korea there. I felt like throwing up. What happened to the lamb's brain?

Fortunately, they said that they hadn't butchered any sheep that day! I was so nervous that I might get forced to eat lamb's brain. As soon as I got in the car, I said teasingly.

"It was unlucky. But I'm glad. Because your mission failed."

It turned out that they serve lamb's brains only to really important guests in Central Asia... I thought they were just trying to make fun of me at the time, I'm sorry Dashka!

I left Zamiin-Uud after watching the Copa América Cup match between Argentina and Chile. After the game, I got ready to go to the Gobi Desert. I told you earlier that I saw a post of a Korean blogger that I bought a box of bottled water and went to the Gobi Desert. I thought it would be hard for me to carry that much water, so I bought six 1.5 liters (9 liters) of them and tried to load them on my bicycle, and said Baija, who was watching next to me.

"Six is too much. It's only too heavy. You can get to the next town, Sainshand, with just two bottles."

Huh? Someone took a box of small water bottles, and two bottles are enough?

"The Korean I saw on the blog said he took a lot."

"Two bottles are enough. Trust me."

"Dashka! Is that for real?"

"Yes, we only took that much when we rode our bicycles, but since it's your first time, I think you will need just four bottles." Then Baija said again.

"No, four bottles too are heavy. Three bottles are enough!"

"It's my first time, so I'll take four." "It's heavy. You'll want to throw them away on the way."

Then Dashka cut in again.

"No, it's your first time, so I think four bottles would be enough. By the way, do you have any self-defense supplies? Like a gun or a whistle."

"No, I don't even have a knife yet, and I was thinking about going to Russia to buy it. Why?"

"Hey, there are many wolves and wild animals in the desert, and you are not even going to prepare for that?"

"That's okay. I can deal with at least one. I have a hammer and a saw in my toolbox, so that'll be enough."

Dashka nodded reluctantly and said, "It would be dangerous. If you really are, do as you wish."

After all the talks, I got ready to go to the Gobi Desert. Finally, I said goodbye to my friends one by one, took a picture with Dashka's mother, and got on the bicycle to the desert.

Dashka and Baija left home with me, offering to take me to the entrance to the Gobi Desert. Even though we had spent a short time together, I could feel the deep friendship from them, and it was a happy time. And I was able to learn the basic Mongolian language. I think this will remain to me as a precious memory in my life that will be really hard to forget.

When I first realized that I had to cross the Gobi Desert in China, I said to myself, "It's still the beginning of my journey, so I can just keep going," but I couldn't escape the pressure and anxiety that the word desert gave me. However, as I met Dashka who encountered me like a luck and as I stayed there together for three days, I was able to get out of that anxiety and calm down. When I left Dashka's house and pedalled toward the desert, my anxiety and doubts completely disappeared, and I even felt the excitement that I was traveling to the desert. The path I was going to pass like any other ones. I was filled only with a positive mind.

I sent Dashka and Baijoa back and I pedalled to the desert by myself. Now I'm entering the Gobi Desert. I'm starting a real adventure.

On the Gobi Desert

I'm riding the Gobi Desert now. It's not as hot as I thought. And it's not hard either. The good thing is that there hasn't been a sandstorm so far. Dashka said that I can never ride the bicycle when it's windy. He told me to go into the big drain and take a rest if there is a sandstorm. It was not a sandstorm, but I did encounter a few strong winds. At that time, it feels like it would be faster to walk. But if I keep riding, the wind calms down, and I become able to ride well again.

There are no mountains or high hills in the desert, so the view seems to be open for about 20 kilometres. I can see the movement of the clouds well too. Especially the movement of the rain clouds. I can predict it myself by looking at those clouds while riding my bicycle.

"Oh, there's going to be a good shower soon."

Then there goes the shower soon as I expected. It's okay to ride in the rain. The atmosphere is very dry, so even if I ride for an hour or two in the shower, my underwear dries up.

That was when I encountered a localized shower. I had used to show my professional spirit of leaving photos even in dangerous situations, but unfortunately, I had forgotten to take videos.

Anyway, the localized shower I encountered was different from the colour of the clouds. Completely black clouds. I thought that I had to shelter myself into the drain this time when I sensed, "I'm going to meet that shower cloud in at least 10 minutes." I felt something strange. So I pulled my bicycle out to the nearest sewer, and I thought, "It's going to fall for about half an hour and end."

It was a light idea to sit down in the drain and take a rest while it was raining. The shower clouds came closer and closer, and before it started to rain, extremely thick hails began falling. After about 15 minutes of hail, it began to rain slowly. And the sky was completely dark gray. The dark blackish gray clouds covered the sky. "It's falling good." About 20 minutes after sitting in the drain watching the shower? The rain began to pour harder and harder, and now the water started to flow into the drain where I was avoiding the rain. I sat on my bicycle first, leaning against the wall of the drain so that I wouldn't fall. Until then, I was sure the rain would stop soon. But goodness! The water started to fill up, and a one-third of the tires were submerged, but the rain wouldn't think of stopping. While I was on my bicycle, I changed my sneakers to slippers and prayed desperately, desperately for the rain to stop. Because the water was as cold as ice water, my body began to tremble like a leaf as my body temperature began to drop. The water rose higher and higher, and I was afraid that if the rain continued, I would run the risk of the water blowing rapidly and being swept away, but there was no other place to avoid the rain.

Fortunately, God helped me. The rain started to stop. I got wet and climbed up the slope with my heavy bicycle. Full of watery mud and slippery slippers, and when I pulled my bicycle up the road with all my force, it was like I had become Andy, the main character who escaped in the sewer in the movie "The Shawshank Demolition."

As soon as I got on the road, I shovelled the roll cake and chocolate into my mouth as the emergency food. My body temperature went down, and I had run out of energy, so I would have blacked out if I didn't eat the sweets, and it wasn't until I shovelled sugar in my mouth that I was able to get back on my bicycle.

Even if you get wet, it dries up quickly after the sun rises, so you might think that there will be no problem if you just continue riding as usual. But it's even more dangerous because occasionally, there are cars that graze by regardless of whether I can ride the bicycle in the rain or not. There's a high risk of getting killed because of the heavy rain and that they can't see me because they really can't see a few meters ahead in this rain.

Another time I was really scared of is when I was chased by a herd of wild dogs. There are so many wild animals in the desert. Wild horses, cows, camels, and wild dogs… I call them crazy dogs. The crazy dogs run around in groups, and I once ran into those crazy dogs on a road. When I first saw them from a distance, it looked like faint dots. And then as I got closer to them, I began to see them in detail, and when I found out what was going on, I found out that three wild dogs were hunting a cow and digging its intestines. If I knew the situation, I had to get away quickly. But as if I didn't know what a human being is like or how I was like, ignoring the instinctive warning that I had to avoid it quickly, I was watching the bloody scene as if I was on a safari, and at some point, I was finally disturbed by the sight of a wild dog that was in the midst of eating. The moment I felt our eye contact in the air, I unwittingly said, "Oh, I'm screwed." I could read the dog's thoughts by looking at the light of its eyes.

"Oh, that's our dessert."

Frightened out of my wits, I started pedalling at great speed. Pedalling madly in the spirit of a mouse being chased by crazy dogs and a cat after stopping eating and running to eat dessert!

I was lucky again this time. It was such a relief. A large truck that rarely passes by honked its horn before it passed me, and the terrified crazy dogs got scared and ran away, putting an end to the chase between the crazy dogs and a human being on a bicycle, and I was so grateful for the truck at the time that normally wouldn't have been so pleasant. If it weren't for that truck, would I have escaped the fate of being the crazy dogs' dessert like the hunted cow? I don't know. It wasn't until I realized Dashka's words that I must take self-defense weapons wasn't meant to scare me.

Then did I buy a self-defense weapon later? No, not really!

The sky of the Gobi Desert was so clean. The sky was showing a very dark blue colour that I couldn't find a grain of fine dust. It's almost navy. If you look at the sky in Seoul, ot which they always show fine dust warnings on every news on TV, and when you look at the sky in the desert, it's phenomenal. So after a day's ride, you find a flat place, set up a tent, and after dinner, it becomes about 8pm. Then there's nothing more to do.

There was no internet and no friends. At that time, I relieved my loneliness by reading "Don Quixote" that I brought from Korea. The book was so thick that I believed I could be with it until the end of the trip. "Don Quixote" was not only for reading, but it was so thick that it served as a pillow.

When I read "Don Quixote" like that, the sun went down, and I slept in the tent because I could no longer do anything when the sun went down. It was to live with nature.

It was dawn. I don't know exactly what time it was, but I really wanted to go to the bathroom, so I opened the tent and went outside. I was surprised when I looked at the sky unintentionally. I was ecstatic too. As if I feel like I'm on the moon or floating in space? Even if I could combine and multiply all the stars I've seen in my life, it would have been much less than the stars above my head. I went to the bathroom and even after I came back to the tent, I lay in my sleeping bag and looked at the night sky with the tent open. I just stared at the sky for about 15 minutes without thinking. Then I could feel tears pouring down my cheeks. I don't know why my tears welled up so much at that time. Was it because of the touching scenery? After that, I often slept with the tent open. I wanted to capture the stars who came to me secretly when I woke up.

Deserts are a series of uphill and downhill. It was shocking. There are no uphill paths as long as the Great Wall, but the slope seems to be worse in the deserts than in the Great Wall. As I climbed uphill, I spat out all the swear words, and I ran in mind control, saying, "I'm the one who climbed the Great Wall!" Fortunately, there is an end to the uphill, and there is a flat road or downhill behind it. That's all I'm thinking about. Oh, right. One time, I was climbing uphill, and there was a Mongolian car passing by, opening the window and clapping. Of course, I didn't understand it, but I was encouraged because I was sure that it was to cheer me up.

The car waited for me to come up from the shoulder at the top of the uphill, and then the driver put his thumbs up and handed me a small bottle of orange juice. Although it may be a small gift, it still remained in my memory probably because the orange juice was the first gift I ever got on the road.

By the way, the song I listened to the most while I was going through the desert was Kim Bo-kyung's "Don't Think You're Alone." I rode my bicycle barely listening to music after I lost my Bluetooth speaker in China, but I thought of it while I was riding in the desert alone, and I just wanted to listen to that song. Anyway, I have two more days in the desert, and I'm going to Ulaanbaatar, the capital of Mongolia. There were dangerous situations, but it wasn't as bad as I feared. There were days when the sun was very hot, and there were days when there was the right amount of shower that fell for me to cool down, and there were many cloudy days. I think the weather generally helped me a lot while I was passing the desert.

In Ulaanbaatar with Genghis Khan

I passed the vast Gobi Desert and now arrived at Ulaanbaatar. The first place I visited after the arrival was the statue of Genghis Khan. Genghis Khan, whom I learned in history class when I was in middle and high school. It was all my knowledge that he led Mongolian warriors, the nomads accustomed to horsemanship, and ruled the greatest empire in the world's history. I searched for Genghis Khan while pedalling to Ulaanbaatar, saw a famous saying he left, and there were a lot of cool phrases. This was the one I liked the most.

"I didn't know how to write my name, but I learned to be wise by listening to others."

When I was in middle school, I learned about listening to others while reading a book called "Momo." But Genghis Khan learned to be wise beyond listening, so I could see how carefully he listened to others. If you listen carefully to what others say and think about it again, you will be able to make wise judgments about what is right.

I liked another phrase.

"I became Genghis Khan the moment I overcame myself."

It's hard to explain exactly how I felt from this phrase, but I thought they were powerful words anyway.

"The moment I overcame myself…"

Reading and thinking about Genghis Khan's famous sayings one by one, I felt that he was a person who had the capacity and ability to dominate the Great Empire.

That was why I first visited the Genghis Khan statue in Genghis Khan Square after arriving in Ulaanbaatar.

It's been hundreds of years since he passed away, but I kept him in mind and wanted to be like him. And I was pedalling my bicycle towards Europe, where he had ridden a horse and fought wars of conquest with his warriors.

I've never been to the door of the Blue House in my life in Korea. But I actually went to the residence of the President of Mongolia in Ulaanbaatar. This was really a strange thing that happened to me as a result of coincidence. There was nothing much to do except to find the statue of Genghis Khan during my stay in Ulaanbaatar. On the second day, when I looked around the city and went back to the hostel, I met a friend from Lithuania, and she said that she was going to a mountain across from Ulaanbaatar the next day, so I asked her if I could go with her, and she was happy to say yes. The friend, who left her company in Lithuania, said that she was traveling around the world teaching English for free and getting room and board offers.

The next morning, I headed towards the mountain with my friend, and it wasn't easy to get to the entrance of the mountain. We were able to enter a rural village by a minibus and go back to the entrance of the mountain by taxi. They even charged an entrance fee because it's a national park. I felt a bit uneasy when the expense returned as a considerable amount of money after thinking lightly, "Should I give it a try up the mountain?" The tail could not wag the dog. This was a pretty big loss in my little pocket as a long-term traveller. It wasn't hard to get to the top anyway. The scenery was like the ordinary mountains in Korea, but on the summit, an old couple from Italy were sunbathing. They had come to Mongolia from Milan by a trailer. They invited us to their dinner in the trailer, saying that they have good ingredients and homemade tomato sauce that they made. It was a great opportunity to eat their traditional Italian lasagna. I couldn't refuse. I really wanted to accept their invitation. But damn it! The friend I went with just wanted to go back to Ulaanbaatar. What can I do? I was sorry, but I had to follow her decision because I was the one who jumped into her plan.

As I mentioned earlier, I'm just a poor traveller who has to complete a long trip with little money. So I had to save money when I could. From the top of the mountain, the downtown of Ulaanbaatar looked right in front of us. There is no way, but I thought that we could save money by going down to the visible Ulaanbaatar compared to going down the trail where we went up. Of course, it requires some adventurous spirit and the consent of the partner. We were both thinking the same thing. The adventure began. Each of us only had our own cell phone, a small water bottle, and a filter for the water purifier.

When we went down the mountain for the first time, there was a trace of the trail, so we could go down without any problems. The path was arranged like a trail according to each section, and they were marked on the trees, so we just had to follow it down. But as we entered a certain section, the signs and traces of people suddenly disappeared. Every time, we looked at the map on our cell phone and went down to see where Ulaanbaatar was, and then there were signs on the rocks and trees, so as we had started going down the mountain at about three, we thought that we could get to Ulaanbaatar by six or seven. But goodness! It didn't take a long time to realize that we were lost in the mountain. We had already run out of water to drink. My friend scooped up the stream water into the water filter and drank it, but I held back from it because I could get an upset stomach.

Was it around 8pm? On the map of our cell phone, it looked like we had almost come down the mountain, but goodness! Far from downtown Ulaanbaatar, only the ridges of the mountain kept appearing. Then we could see that some buildings were located close to us with some parking lot signs on the map. We walked toward the buildings. There was no hiking trail, but we went there because we wanted to get out of the mountain before sunset.

After many twists and turns, the time we succeeded in climbing down the mountain was around 9:45pm. We washed ourselves briefly in the stream and headed to the buildings. We met a family in the parking lot of the building who had just returned from shopping, the man who looked like a husband looked amazed at how we were there, and we walked up to them first because we thought that we could come up with some solutions. We asked them if they could call us a taxi.

The man said that the place was where taxis are not allowed. There are roads for cars to pass by, and there is a parking lot, but is he saying that taxis can't come in? So we asked him if he could take us to the place where we could take a taxi, but instead, he handed us bottles of some beverage, saying that he will call other people who can help us.

A few minutes later, some people came to help us, and they were three extraordinary-looking soldiers and one commander in charge of them. We were captured by the soldiers, driven to the checkpoint, and the commander told us that this was the residence of the Mongolian president. It was that we had trespassed into the residence of the Mongolian president without permission. We wondered what the chances are of ending up coming down to this place after climbing down a mountain.

Starting with the inspection of our belongings at the checkpoint, we each described how we came across the mountain, and we were interrogated by Russian and Korean-speaking interrogators. We hadn't done anything wrong, so we didn't feel intimidated. We received the interrogations in a dignified manner. But on the other hand, I also thought of a fluke, "Wouldn't they take us to a hostel when they're done?"

When all the procedures were over, the time was already past 1:30am, and fortunately, the people who interrogated us took us to a hostel. We were very tired, but we had achieved our goal of saving transportation costs, and we had made an unforgettable memory of invading the residence of the Mongolian president. It was a day we went to bed somewhat contentedly.

A Meaningful Volunteer Work, Ugii Nuur

I planned to go to Lake Baikal in Russia directly from Ulaanbaatar, but since I had visited with a 60-day Mongolian visa, it felt like it was a bit of a waste and sad to leave Mongolia in just a few weeks. Then Lake Khövsgöl came to my mind, which my Mongolian friend Dashka had recommended me to go to. So I made plans to go to Lake Khövsgöl via Tsetserleg and turned the steering wheel.

I went out of Ulaanbaatar, rode for a long time, passed the fork, and after 10 kilometres of uphill and downhill, I checked the map. It was a sad news that I had to go in a different direction from the fork for the shortest distance, but luckily, I only had to go around 10 kilometres, so I kept my energy and went back to where the fork was.

There was a rest area near the fork. There was no sign here, but it seemed like it was written, "This is the last rest area," so I thought I should have a full lunch first and take a rest. When I entered the store with no particular worry, there was a restaurant on one side and a small supermarket on the other.

First, I went into the supermarket, got a cold beer from the refrigerator, came over to the restaurant, and ordered food. Of course I had a beer before the food came out. The cool beer moistened my throat freshly. It felt like as if the energy I had wasted by taking the wrong way was being recharged. I felt like it wasn't enough, so I bought another beer and drank it with the food that was served. It was a delicious meal with beer while sitting in the cool shade, getting away from the blazing sun and the asphalt that was heated like an iron plate where meats are grilled. It was such a sweet break.

I got on my bicycle after resting for a while after I finished my meal, and after about 10 minutes since I started pedalling. Maybe because of the hot weather, I was starting to get tipsy. My body loosened languidly, and my eyelids sank. All the tissues and organs in my body asked me to just lie on the ground. I looked for a shade, but there were only faint traces of the clouds in the shade. I ran with all my might, but I soon reached my limit, and I said, "Oh well! I don't know!" and I left my bicycle on the side of the road and lied down on the street. It didn't matter what happened next.

Did I sleep for about 10 minutes? I woke up because it was so hot that I was burning to death, but I felt like I had sobered up and became fine.

It was a dizzy experience. I couldn't believe that I lain spread-eagled on the street. I was so shocked that after that, I decided to abstain from alcohol when I ride a bicycle. It was fortunate that nothing had happened.

I rode the same road the next day. Lavender flowers blooming on the side of the road were seen here and there. And after riding a little bit more, there were now much more lavender flower beds and a scenery where sheep and goats were having a meal. My heart had become peaceful and ecstatic. But as I loved the scenery in front of me so much that I prepared to take a picture with the sheep, the flock of sheep and goats ran away far away. Eventually, I couldn't take pictures. But it was a source of comfort that I could keep in my eyes. If I could go there again someday, wouldn't I be able to see the scenery that was like a dream again?

I looked at the map before I got back on my bicycle, and it was right that the way I was going was the shortest route to Tsetserleg, but when I looked closely, I found out that it was not the main road. In Mongolia, the fact that it is not the main road means that the asphalt road will end soon. However, I didn't want to go back the way that I had been riding for more than a day, so I rode with expectations just in case. As I had expected, the road was connected to an unpaved road. My bicycle was made to fit the paved road. On some unpaved roads, the ground was flat and hard, so it was okay, but in some sections, no matter how hard I pedalled, it didn't move forward properly. This was because the unpaved roads in Mongolia were made of sand, and they were bumpy like a washboard. Riding on such an unpaved road for an hour is harder than riding on a paved road for more than three hours.

I couldn't go back, so I had no choice but to go forward. While I was desperately struggling pedalling, I saw something unexpected in front of me. It was a sign in Korean.

"Ugii Nuur Forest: 16 kilometres"

Wow~ It was a hope that came like a miracle. That day's destination was definitely that place. Hanging a Korean sign meant that there were Koreans there. I felt like I could wash, sleep, and get food if I arrived there, and the energy that I had lost came back.

In front of the village was a large signboard called "Ugii Nuur Forest." Behind the signboard was a vinyl greenhouse that are common in Korea, and I could see Mongolians working there. I blindly approached them and initiated a conversation. I don't remember how I spoke in detail, but I had probably pointed at myself and shouted, "Korea! Korea!" One of them guided me to the house where the Korean volunteers lived as if he understood what I said. Really, I couldn't believe that I met Koreans in such a remote place. Even they seemed surprised to see me. It was probably because they had never dreamed that a Korean tourist would come by riding a bicycle.

Although I couldn't stay there for a long time, I had a really meaningful time making food and participating in volunteer work together. Before I started the journey, I had said to myself, "If there becomes somewhere that needs my help while I travel, let me not just pass by," and that was where it was. I couldn't be of much help, but I was happy just to be able to help. The people who come all the way to the countryside like this and doing volunteer work. It came to my mind that there are so many good people around the world.

As I tried to leave the road again, they worried that I had to go 120 kilometres to get to Tsetserleg and 50 kilometres on the unpaved road. But I wasn't worried so much because I had filled my body and mind with energy. It was because the road will eventually come to an end, and I just had to pedal.

Jerome, My First Riding Partner

I left Ugii Nuur Forest on an unpaved road by myself. There were paved roads and several routes on the map, but it wasn't easy to actually find them. What would the joy of finding a paved road after being lost several times equal to? When I was dreaming of riding on a flat asphalt road that I would meet for the first time in a long time, some Mongolians near the paved road waved to me. Now that the path of hardship was over, I approached them to take a rest. They told me, "Your friend here!"

"There is a Korean here?"

They pointed silently at a bicycle on a car.

At that time, a friend greeted me. It was Jerome. My first riding friend. It was like I met a soulmate. When it began to shower again, Jerome left for Tsetserleg in a Mongolian's car, saying that he was too tired. I had planned to go camping before entering Tsetserleg the next day, so we decided to meet in Tsetserleg and parted. But when the rain that I thought was a shower didn't stop, I couldn't dare to camp and went to the Tsetserleg guest house that Jerome had told me. Jerome wasn't in the guest house. Moreover, all the reservations were full, so there were no beds left. I texted Jerome, but there was no answer, so I had no choice but to go into the hotel right next to me, and there was a bicycle parked in the hotel's lobby. I had a feeling that soulmates could work together as expected.

I was looking forward to it when I pedalled with Jerome at first. I thought that we could share conversations and relieve boredom. But the reality was different. Once we got on the bike, silence came, and we ended up going our own ways, back and forth. There was no difference between having a partner and not having one.

But it's really different that there's someone who can rest together, eat together in the evening, set up a tent, and sleep together. The companion who rides his bicycle at his own speed but eats and talks together when gets off the bicycle. That means more than you think.

Jerome was a friend who started his trip from Paris. He said that his goal is to go to Turkey through the Balkan Peninsula and to Japan via Central Asia. He was on the opposite path to me, who was now only at the beginning of the trip, and he was running in the second half of his trip.

I thought that the camping supplies I had were everything until I met Jerome. So I was surprised when I looked inside Jerome's tent. An air mattress and an air pillow. These two things were totally new to me. When Jerome slept on the air pillow, I slept with Don Quixote as a pillow. I was content not to sleep cold in a thick sleeping bag that I had bought in China when Jerome laid down on a soft air mattress. As soon as I saw Jerome's camping equipment, I felt as if I had become a medieval man who saw a cultured person.

There are many unforgettable vivid memories between him and me. Over dinner, we always promised to get up at seven in the morning, and at seven the next morning, we'd stick out each other's faces and go back into the tent with conversations like "30min more?" and "Of course!" We never woke up at seven as we had promised. And Jerome used to make jokes when we got off to a fresh start and when the wind started blowing.

"Do you want to go back?"

Coming to think of it now, I wonder why such a small joke was so much fun then. It was the same that we liked lame jokes that we always took out during the breaks and mealtimes. My first riding partner who hit every little detail right. That was Jerome.

It was when I was riding in front. A Mongolian who approached me on a horse from far away suggested to me that he would swap his horse and my bicycle. I had never ridden a horse, but I gladly accepted his offer because I felt that I would regret it if I didn't ride the horse even though I had come all the way to Mongolia.

But when I was about to put my foot into the stirrup hanging from the saddle to ride the horse, it realized that the person who was trying to get on its back wasn't its owner, so I raised my front feet, and it ran away. Of course I couldn't get on the horse. Maybe it was fortunate that I couldn't ride the horse. But all of a sudden, when the horse ran away, the owner looked as if he had lost his country, and he started to trudge to find his horse, having never stepped on my pedal. I was sorry for nothing. After that, I completely gave up on riding a Mongolian horse.

Jerome said that he cooked pasta or other dishes every evening since the first day of his traveling. When I heard that, I tilted my head. "How could you bother doing that every day?"

"It's nothing. Of course, you have to cook food to eat." But Jerome also confessed that he had experienced a new world when he first experienced Chinese ramen. He said that he often ate Chinese ramen for dinner because Chinese ramen was fast, convenient, and had fewer dishes, but his cooking skills remained the same, and the French tomato pasta that he had made the day before we parted in Hövsgöl was really delicious. Jerome's tomato pasta, which was usually made with the ingredients available at the Mongolian mart and his camping supplies, had an unforgettable taste. It seemed simple at first glance, but I think that the French taste was hidden in such simplicity.

We rode together for a week, and for five days of that, we rode on unpaved roads. If I were alone, I would never have run on unpaved roads. It is very difficult to ride a bicycle in Mongolia because the soil is close to sand. But it was so nice to have someone I could ride with, and someone I could rest with after a hard climb uphill.

We parted at Hövsgöl. Now I'll pedal to England, and he'll pedal to Japan. Jerome, who was studying archaeology, said that he had been attending a vocational college to work as a nurse after this trip. As I parted with him, I hoped that everything he had wanted would go well, and I wished him well. If I ever go to Paris, France, I want to ride my bike again to eat the baguette that Jerome boasted about so much.

Bye, Mongolia!

Lake Hövsgöl is connected to Lake Baikal of Russia. This means that that's how far I'm up close to Russia right now. I wanted to move to Russia from Hövsgöl, but the owner of the guesthouse in Lake Hövsgöl told me that there is a border immigration office in Hövsgöl, but only for Mongolian and Russians. It was a bolt out of the blue. I had no choice but to go back the way I had come from Ulaanbaatar to Lake

Hövsgöl and go to the border open to foreigners. I was so angry. It was because if the weather gets cold, it will become harder to pass through Siberia. I was in a hurry, and it was three days later after I managed to get to the last city of Mongolia by riding 150 kilometres or 160 kilometres a day.

There was an interesting incident on the way to the last city in Mongolia. I encountered a shuttle bus that I had seen wandering around in Seoul. At first, I thought that it was just because Mongolia is a country that imports a lot of used cars. But I thought, "Interesting," so I tried to take a picture of the bus standing on the side of the road, and I heard a familiar language.

"Aren't you Korean?"

That was it. I was sure that a Mongolian was driving it, but I was wrong. He told me that three Koreans were traveling around the world by the shuttle bus. The bus was so remodelled that it could go anywhere in the world. The back of the bus had a mosquito net and a mattress for three people to sleep, a luggage compartment in the front, and extra seats for the hitch hikers they happened to meet. It was a bus full of romantic vibes. Coming to think of it, it comes to my mind that there are so many people who enjoy traveling in various ways now.

It's been a month since I travelled in Mongolia. I was supposed to pass it in about a week, but I pedalled in Mongolia for three more weeks, which means that the time I should have passed Siberia has been postponed for another three weeks. That means that I might have to endure the cold that much more, but I don't regret changing my original plan. I was able to make more friendships and memories with Mongolians, and I also met a soulmate who rode with me together. The beautiful Mother Nature of Mongolia that I had captured with my eyes was a bonus.

Travelling in Mongolia gets me so many invitations. If there's a Ger near the street, they'll definitely come out and invite me to their house. I don't know how they find me, but they run to me from quite far away, invite me to their house, and recommend milk tea, Mongolian cheese, snacks, etc. The milk tea had a peculiar taste of water mixed with fresh milk, which was quite addictive, and the cheese was pretty good. Jerome liked it very much because it was delicious. After eating the snacks they had prepared, they gave me a bowl of Mongolian meat noodles, even though it wasn't even time for dinner yet. So I sometimes used to look for where Ger was when there was about to be a shower.

But there are a few things to keep in mind when you are invited. There are many Mongolians who often tell you to drink together and ask you to sleep at their home. But if you think that they drank too much, I recommend that you sleep in a separate tent from Ger because you don't know how they'll change when they become drunk. Even if that's not the case, I recommend that you use a personal sleeping bag when sleeping in bed in Ger.

This is because once I slept with their blankets on, I almost went crazy because my whole body went itchy the next day. Oh! And it's always a good idea to bring extra snacks like roll cakes with you just in case of invitations. This is because you can show them your wit in giving gifts to the children of the owner of the house who invited you.

One word that never got out of my head while riding in the Mother Nature of Mongolia for a month was 'Cleanness.' The near-transparent clear skies, clear rivers, groups of shiny stars… and the pure hearts of the Mongolian people.

Now I'm leaving Mongolia to go to Russia. It's the country where I will have to spend the most time on my trip.

Take care, Mongolia!

Tips Bike Tour in Mongolia

Self-Defense Items

The vast Gobi Desert might seem empty, but it's wild and holds surprises. I ignored Daschka's advice about carrying self-defense gear until I had a wild run-in with desert dogs.

So, if you're cautions unlike me, pack some protection.

Gobi's Unpredictable Weather

The Gobi isn't just about animal remnants; it's hotspot for rain/sand storms too. You'll face a choice – brave it or find shelter. Those giant drainage pipes unexpectedly become your refuge from the desert's tantrums.

No Alcohol

Imagine pedalling through a Gobi or Greenland oven. Sun, asphalt, and heat. A cold drink, maybe even a beer, becomes a dream. I learned the hard way not to down a lunch beer. Riding on, it hit me hard. The heated asphalt was only one place to have a rest.

Save the beer for dinner!

Little Present for Kid

Life on the road brings unexpected bonds. Welcomed into a Ger, I shared warmth and hospitality. In return, I gave kids cakes—every day for me, extraordinary for them. It's the little gestures that cross cultures and create the best memories.

From Asia to Europe: Russia

Still in Ulan-Ude, Mongolia

I thought that people had to get on a car just in the case of moving from China to Mongolia, but getting on a car should be done when going from Mongolia to Russia.

I did not know for sure.

As I got to the border checkpoint of Mongolia by bicycle, the police working there kindly made a truck stop to take me.

I was able to cross the border after loading my bicycle on the truck.

Vehicle inspections at Russian checkpoint are stricter than when crossing from China to Mongolia. When they inspected cars, they basically opened the bonnet and trunk to get all the luggage off to do some inspection. But when they inspected the trucks, they really inspected too thoroughly.

For sure, the vehicles whose drivers wanted to cross the border had to wait in line for a long time, otherwise, it is not that meticulous to inspect entrants.

When I had crossed from China into Mongolia, I went to a separate checkpoint and got immigration procedures.

But crossing from Mongolia to Russia, we did not have to get off from the car and just passed our passport to get the stamp.

The truck I was on was also inspected. There was nothing there except for my bicycle. They did not check it thoroughly.

They just asked me some questions like "do you have drugs or firearms," and ended the inspection. I was able to enter Russia more easily than I thought.

A Russian I had met in Mongolia said that there is no need to learn the Russian language because there are so many people in Russia who can speak English.

I blindly believed his words and crossed the border without worrying. But I had difficulty in communication, contrary to what I expected. Students can speak a little English, but not as many people as I expected.

I made one rule that was; staying the night in the border city on the day of crossing the border. Because it is hard to pedal a lot on that day.

The very day after crossing the border, I met a student riding a bicycle and asked about a proper place for me to set up my tent, and he guided me to a place like a sports complex.

After that, I even asked the security guide if I could set a tent there and he allowed me to do that, even to wash in the building facility and sleep comfortably on a couch.

It was a moment when Russia's image was definitely upgraded for me.

I had some free time to exercise for running and gymnastics on the playground, I saw 5 people playing volleyball on the court.

Of course, I approached them to ask whether I could play together. They were willing to allow me to join.

Were they local student athletes? They were really good players.

You know that doing something with people for fun, like a hobby, makes me concentrate more on enjoying, than that with people doing well.

I felt like that.

Once again, I felt gratitude towards myself who loved sports. Exercise makes people get along with ease.

The second day after entering Russia was a day full of surprises with new things.

I met only one cyclist while pedalling all the way to Russia, but I met a Japanese and three guys from Switzerland.

The Japanese used to load lots of stuff on their bikes to the extent that it felt weird.

But you can imagine them if you thought they travelled with the way before a lot of bicycle accessories were invented, a decade or two ago.

It was loaded in such classic method.

In other words, it could seem a little shabby.

The more I looked, the more I wondered how it was possible to travel with so much luggage on his bicycle.

Anyway, he was so kind.

I didn't ask him but he gave me lots of information about Russia.

For example, which road sections were not in good condition, that I should register for entry to check-in hotel, where a store was located, how I could get a bottle of water at a restaurant in a hurry …. things like these.

One of the most pleasant pieces of information was that he saw two Chinese cyclists in the same direction with me yesterday.

I had an expectation that I might have a companion on my riding trip together once again.

On the other hand, the three men from Switzerland, over 65 years of age, prepared lots of bicycle items to put on their bicycles which were incomparable to the other cyclists from Japan; they had bicycle accessories, and even the latest GPS.

I felt that if the Japanese traveller was like a person who travelled on a riding trip from the past, or 10 years ago, those from Switzerland were like people who travelled on a riding trip from the present, or about 5 years from the future.

They let me see the map showing their trace from Switzerland. It was so amazing. Age is not important, but passion and putting in action what you want to do is.

This is the point that we should look up to.

I asked them about the Chinese cyclists whom they had seen, and they answered that they had seen them about 30 kilometres ago.

Wow, I was so happy to think that I could catch up with them and pedal together! It took one more day to meet them.

And I rode with them all the way to Ulan-Ude together.

On the way to Ulan-Ude, my rear wheel burst for the first time since I had started the trip. It was because of the broken vodka bottles that were scattered on the road.

Not only did the tube burst, but the tire had to be replaced because a piece of glass pierced one the side of the tire.

I brought a spare tire, but was hoping it wouldn't happen... The spare tire was so thin that it was likely to puncture easily. But what can you do?

I had no choice but to park my bike on the roadside and do the repairs. It was my first experience changing tubes and tires.

Seeing my Chinese friends waiting for me made me more impatient and nervous.

I didn't even check if it was properly inserted or not, and just pushed it back in and started to pedal again.

Sadly, it burst again because either they didn't sit properly or the tube was stuck inside.

There were about 3 kilometres left till we reached the hostel in Ulan-Ude, so I decided to fix it at the accommodation, and took my bicycle; repeatedly refilling the window to the tires until I got to the hostel.

Of course, at the hostel, when the last remaining spare tube was carefully replaced, I made a mistake. When we get impatient and act hastily in anything, we get ruined.

There is a saying that the more you are in a hurry, the more you should go back.

At first, we were going to stay in Ulan-Ude for just one day and leave straight to Lake Baikal. Since there was no spare tube for me and I was worried about pedalling with spare tires, so I decided to fix the bike and then set off, which made me stay one more day.

But even though I visited a couple of bike shops, I could not find the right tubes for my bike.

To make matters worse, on the way to the bike shop, the wire on the rear gear shifter broke.

In this situation, I did not have any wires to work with for my bike, so I had no choice but to just fix it as a temporary fix.

I had no choice but to quickly go to a big city, named Irkutsk.

I wondered if I could get to Irkutsk without repairing the tire and broken gear shifter.

It was over 500 kilometres from Ulan-Ude to Irkutsk, and on the way if my tire burst, I would be totally done.

I took a walk concerning it in the afternoon.

Should I take a train or just keep pedalling my bicycle, following my fate? I finally decided to do it as long as I could.

Once I would do my best and if the situation is not possible to last, then I would get on a train.

My Bucket List, Lake Baikal

I had lots of fun things from arriving in Irkutsk and staying there.

I put the spare tire on my front wheel and biked without a spare tube for bike, with Chinese cyclists leaving Irkutsk.

To Lake Baikal, but I biked a little quickly so we naturally got separated.

I did take a rest for 2 days; I biked listening to an audio book and it didn't make me feel too tired.

I rode my bike like the wind.

Originally, I had planned to get near Lake Baikal to look around the lake and view, but as I got closer to the place, I loved seeing the lake so much that I ended up riding the bike over 150 kilometres. I arrived there at around 7 o'clock.

But there was no place where I could stay to camp and set up my tent. At that moment, I discovered a small town around the place.

I asked two women I met near the town about some place that I could stay for camp, and one of them who looked older invited me to her house.

I visited her place without expectation and one of her family members had been studying in America so we had no problem with communication.

It was a two-storey wooden house, and I could stay in a cosy attic. I was able to have a good night.

The attic had windows in the front and back; from the back side window, I could see the railroad track of the Trans-Siberian Railway, and behind the railroad, Lake Baikal stood out.

It was an awesome scenery.

They offered me a favour and served me fried fish and fish soup after I took a shower. I had no chance to eat fish since leaving Korea, so I really missed it.

When they served me the fish, oh how happy I was.

I had just wanted to know where I could stay for one night, and it got me a cosy bed, and after a long time, I enjoyed a nice supper that was served by the two women.

This time, I could compensate for their favour by eating well.

This is a rare experience except for a tour, actually I had been treated so well by many people from China and Mongolia to Russia.

It feels like treating guests carefully is part of their culture. When I get treated like this, I can feel something. The warm trust between people.

After having dinner, I went to the lake to look around and put my feet in the water.

I had really wanted to visit there, but it was not better than I expected so I was a little disappointed.

I imagined that this lake would be so pure, like feeling transparent, but it wasn't not so clean because of lots of moss.

Anyway, I hoped to visit Lake Baikal and I put my feet on the water and so it means one of my bucket list wishes could be deleted.

When I came back to the house, the women served me some wine and snacks including cheese. We talked together. The host said that she had visited Korea, and the memories in Korea were so good. Koreans were so kind and there were a lot of interesting things, and canned coffee was an amazing invention which was not sold in Russia so she envied us.

Next day, she made me breakfast and also gave me a sandwich and fruits to eat for lunch.

And she gave the phone number of her son to call her when I got to the capital of Russia, Moscow.

I didn't expect to get invited and make these pleasant memories, they also made meals for me to have, even after leaving their house. It was so touching and thankful.

I didn't feel any pain and hardness from riding.

But this happy situation didn't last for a long time.

There were ascent and descent so frequently, and how steep were the slopes!

I was riding the roads; uphill and downhill repeatedly, feeling out of breath. It was the first time I met a Korean who travelled with two wheels.

I was in the middle of going uphill.

It was so hard to get on the climb, and I gasped and a motorcycle came up next to me. Just looking at the people, I could feel they were Korean, and one of them said to me, "You from Korea?"

I took a deep breath and answered so fast.

"Yeah, but can we talk at the top of the hill over there?" Anyone who has ever ridden a bicycle would know.

You would never want to stop halfway on an uphill road.

It's a drug-like attraction that feels like I'm going to die but I keep going as if I got possessed by something.

It's not like competing with others but I feel like I would lose if I take a break in the middle.

I can stop in the middle of the hill to take a break and start riding again, or take my bike, but I don't feel like doing that.

I met the motorcycle traveller again, who waited for me on the top of the hill. He introduced himself as, a photographer named "Kim Han".

We just wanted to take a break, but we had a long time after eating snacks together and talking to one another in Korean.

He said he was going to Irkutsk that day.

It was at least 300 kilometres to Irkutsk, and it was impossible for me to be able to get there the same day. We had to get separated because we had a different destination and route to go to.

To promise to meet again at Irkutsk.

After saying goodbye to him, something that should not have happened came to be.

The colour of the clouds changed and it started to drizzle, and then it started to rain. I met countless times this kind of situation in Mongolia countless times so I just continued to ride.

But, as I kept pedalling, I felt the rear wheel sink, so I checked the back side and something I was worried about had occurred.

The rear wheel was out of air.

It was like the situation when I had entered Ulan-Ude.

When the air got out of the wheel, I put some air in it and repeated several times pedalling to the closest train station.

I remember I kept riding that way for a few kilometres.

But I felt like if I kept going this way, it could even ruin even the wheel which could make things worse. I had no choice but to get off the bicycle to take it.

In the rain, I took a bicycle and walked to the train station for about 10 kilometres. It was so hard.

What made me feel a little sad was, that if I was driving on the road and had met a young man pulling his bicycle in the rain, I would have asked at least once what's going on and if there was anything that I could help with.

But a lot of cars passed by me and they just splashed water.

When I was pedalling, it was not so cold even in the rain, but walking in the rain was really cold. I had on shorts and a short-sleeved tee, so it was hard to keep my body temperature warm.

I was shivering so much in the cold and managed to get to the train station. I thought I should change clothes first.

If I got a cold wearing the wet clothes, I couldn't keep my travelling going.

I couldn't bring my bike on the normal train, but on the train that connected town to town.

To get on the train, I had to wait until next morning, so I had to take fruits that I got in the morning, set up tent inside the train station, and sleep with a wet sleeping bag.

The next day, I woke up early to get on the train, and stopped at another station named Slyudyanka to transfer. When I waited for the other train, I met Korean seniors who had come for a tour.

It was nice to meet the people who came from my country and it felt like meeting my parents when I met them.

After they listened to my travel stories, they encouraged and, praised me, and gave me some snacks. It was a really warm time.

After leaving the station and breaking up with them, I felt bored.

I could have spent time eating snacks that the Koreans gave to me, and reading Don Quixote, but I was already reading all of the thick book….

I didn't reserve a guest house, but stayed in a studio room apartment provided by the family of Polina, a Russian I met in Mongolia for a week in Irkutsk.

That was a present for myself as summer vacation and maintenance time.

I completely repaired my bicycle and bought items that I needed for camping.

A rain jacket in case of rain, an air pillow to replace Don Quixote, and air mattress that I can sleep on, a high quality sleeping bag that is much smaller but better than a Chinese-made one, and one bag in which I can carry all things I bought.

Isn't this enough for a bicycle traveller? It's luxury enough.

I went camping near the Lake Baikal.

I wanted to swim in the lake during the day and enjoy the summer vacation watching movies in my tent.

But the weather was not good enough for swimming and even for reflecting the view of the lake. But I met someone who was really interesting.

He was from Moscow, visiting here for vacation.

He had been doing yoga for the 10 years and eating only raw food, not cooked, as a vegan. I was so curious about what he ate for a living.

He said that he had loved alcohol and parties when he was young. But everyone gets a turning point in life. For him, I.

It was travelling to India that changed his life.

It was a big change in the way he looked at life.

So, he started doing yoga, reduced drinking alcohol and smoking, got vegan to lighten his body and mind, and started drinking tea.

It had been 10 years since he had reduced alcohol, smoking, and eating meat slowly, and it turned to his eating and living style.

There are countless and various people, and their stories are woven so complicatedly.

Travelling and meeting so many people to listen to their footprints, it felt like I was discovering the unknown world and it made me feel so interested.

And I thought carefully to build up my own story from this trip.

1,000 Kilometres to Krasnoyarsk

After leaving Irkutsk, there stands only small villages, literally, in the plains of Siberia. The big city is Krasnoyarsk, which I had to ride about 1,000 kilometres to get to.

The distance was similar to going from Panmunjom to Busan, which is almost the farthest distance in Korea to get between.

Living in Korea, I couldn't feel how far away it was until I left Irkutsk. It took 8 days from Irkutsk to Krasnoyarsk.

So many things happened to me.

On the first day after leaving Irkutsk, I stayed one night in the village named Listvyanka, where I set my tent in an amusement park or something.

Of course, I was allowed to by the manager.

I took a rest after eating and taking a shower, when the manager came to me with three women. They looked like a family. Mother and two daughters.

But, it turned out that the one I thought was the mother and older daughter were friends, and the other woman was the younger sister of the one who I thought was the eldest daughter.

They said that they came to meet me because there were few foreign travellers from Asia in this place, so they felt curious about me.

And they asked me, "Can I hold your hand?"

There was no reason to reject it. We shook hands and took a photo together. It felt like being a star, taking a photo with them.

I arrived at a village named Tulun on the third day.

As I got to the village, I first saw the sports stadium for the very first time.

It was around 5 pm so I wanted to exercise a little and find where to sleep. I exercised by myself.

Some people went with a game of football.

I couldn't stand it because I have a fetish for football balls. (I really love football). So, eventually, I approached them to ask if I could join them to play football together, and they were willing to allow me.

I played football which I had not done it for a long time so I was very excited. To survive in the physical fight with the big Russians, I sweat hard a lot with a deadly, evil spirit.

After finishing the match, we moved to a river to take a shower. It looked like the routine of this town.

I borrowed shower gel and shampoo from them and took a shower, which was the first shower for me after leaving Irkutsk so I felt refreshed like I was flying.

They went to their homes and I set my tent on the playground to sleep, but. They came to me again with vodka and snacks.

There is nothing like football when it comes to getting close to each other and becoming friends. When the small party was over, they gave me vodka as a present.

I was so thankful, but it was too heavy for me to carry.

On the seventh day, around lunchtime, I entered a city named Kansk.

This was not to take a rest or stop by a mart, but to go through the centre of the city, that was about three kilometres shorter than going through the longer way.

I was crossing the centre of the city without looking at the map.

As I was waiting for a traffic light with other cars, someone from the other side ran to me waving his hand.

I thought for a while, 'Who is this person in the city where I know nobody?' but I had been so lonely to ride alone.

It turned out that we met at a rest stop about 4 days ago.

There, I had lunch sitting in front of the rest stop, and he was entering the stop to have lunch with his friends.

He said that he had been going to Lake Baikal by riding a motorcycle for summer vacation. And he came back to his workplace and happened to look at me passing by his store.

He took me to the store and gave me some lunch he had brought from home.

He happened to run a hardware store, so he repaired my bicycle; welding the slightly broken rear luggage rack, and replacing the screws I had changed in Mongolia and tightened them.

It was surprising to meet again in Siberia which is wild and spacious, and I thought that the world is not too wild for us to meet like this.

1,000 kilometres to Krasnoyarsk that I've passed for the past 8 days.

And more than half of the 8 days, it rained all day

If I hadn't bought a rain jacket in Irkutsk, I would have been in a lot of trouble.

When I wore the rain jacket the first time, it was well water proof, like when raindrops on a lotus leaf roll down but it gradually lost its waterproof function. Eventually, on the day I entered Krasnoyarsk, my rain jacket got wet.

There was a place I visited on purpose in Krasnoyarsk.

It was a restaurant named 'Gangnam Chicken'.

I didn't necessarily want to eat chicken.

I did talk about the book Don Quixote that I read for travelling.

It was used as a pillow of course.

I read the thick book so fast because I was too concentrated on the main character, Don Quixote. The time and social circumstances were different but the similar factor was that we both went on an adventure.

Maybe that's why I was so concentrated in reading the book so quickly.

I vividly remember that when I was a child, sometimes I wielded a wooden branch against a fruit tree like an enemy.

Just like Don Quixote rushed to the windmill. Anyway, I read all of the books. because after I finished riding on a day and took a rest, there was nothing that I could do. With no Wi-Fi, there was nothing to enjoy.

That's why I entered the restaurant the very first moment when I arrived in Krasnoyarsk. I thought that I could get a book in Korean there.

On the first visit, the owner of the restaurant was absent so I visited it again on the next day. The owner was a second-generation Korean immigrant but she couldn't speak Korean.

She spoke Russian and a little English.

I asked her if I could exchange my book, Don Quixote, with another book in Korean and she allowed me to get Korean-written books, as many as I wanted, which she had prepared for the interior.

As I looked around, I found the book 'Brida' written by Paulo Coelho.

After reading *'The Alchemist'*, I had liked Coelho's book. So, I chose it without any hesitation.

I got this book to read; feeling happy because I didn't have to struggle with boredom every evening anymore. Without much expectation, I sent someone a short message saying that

I wanted couch surfing: 'Hello, I have come from Korea by bicycle, could I stay at your place for two days?'

The host sent me a reply and I was allowed to couch-surf for the first time. My first host was Dima.

He had been married, had kids, was a vocalist in a rock band, rode a bicycle for his hobby and was vegan. The next day when I arrived at his house, I was sick after being in the rain.

We couldn't talk much so I took medicine and went to sleep early.

I had slept enough and woke up feeling refreshed. and I felt better than the day before.

While having breakfast, Dima said that he was going to ride a bike with his friends that evening, and asked me to go with him.

I would love to join the meeting, thinking that it would take just 1 or 2 hours at most. We had dinner and went out to meet his friends around 10 pm.

It was unusual to go out for a ride at that late hour. Around 11 pm, his friends gathered and the night of madness began.

Some riding in fixie bikes, gathered and raced across the city on a cold Siberian night. They rode between cars in the cold wind.

So, after riding 15 kilometres in 30 minutes, we went to another friend's house to hold a home party for 2 hours, and then we took the bikes again and rode all around Krasnoyarsk.

After riding with them like crazy with them, it was 4 am when we returned to his home. It was the first time I had such fun riding a bike.

On a calm night, racing under the street lights! It felt like my adrenaline was exploding.

The next day, we toured the tourist attractions of Krasnoyarsk with Dima's grandfather and grandaunt, and climbed the most famous mountain in the town. Oh, I said that Dima was vegan; so. Thanks to him, I could try veggie kebabs, and the kebabs were so delicious, made with three different kinds of cheese instead of meat.

Dima introduced me to his musician friend, Roman, in case I go to Novosibirsk to stay in his house.

The Capital of Siberia, Novosibirsk

I was so happy to be able to meet my friends a few days ago.

They looked great having a rooftop party with their girlfriends.

I couldn't attend the party, which was a little disappointing, but just meeting them was satisfying for me.

I don't remember exactly who it was, but someone asked me, "How do you wash yourself, sleeping outside, setting up a tent every day?"

I said to the person that I only brushed my teeth, and washed just my face, hands and feet with wet tissue, and I think he or she looked disappointed.

But, it's the truth.

After that, I came up with a new way to wash.

First, buy a small towel and a water bottle of 2 litres, and then make a small hole in the lid of the water bottle.

It would be used like a one-hole shower head.

Before taking a shower, I first wiped my face with a wet tissue, washed my hair and body by using the two-litre portable shower, and then dried my body with a small, newly-bought towel.

After washing like this and laying in my tent, I felt really refreshed.

Then, perhaps because of the freshness from washing my body, when I woke up, I felt definitely reduced fatigue than the other days. *Why hadn't I thought of this before?*

Later, I made another way to save water to buy, and it was that before starting to camp, it is better to enter the last village.

There is an old water pump for common use in most villages, where I could get some water for the day's shower.

The more I travelled, the more I evolved.

When I rode alone on the spacious lands of Siberia, I should.

At that time, I used to ride looking at the speedometer to reduce the boredom. The unit I had was miles, so the speedometer showed up to 999.99 miles.

The thrill of hitting 999.99 and setting it back to 0, was similar to the feeling of completing and submitting a difficult assignment when I was in University. And then, in my head, I roughly calculated the distance that I had to go to in the future.

Murmuring like this: 'I had set it up about 3 times, and around 7 times setting it would be left to complete. Whew, it's so tough."

When I still felt bored, then I pedalled, feeling happy about looking at the changing number of metres.

I felt a thrill of seeing the movement from 10 to 100 digits and accomplished to see it resetting from 999.99 to 0.

At that time, I thought that 'It's not a big deal now but would be a precious memory later', but I couldn't find it on my phone.

I may remove it.

Now that I think about the past, I rode for such little fun and joy, but I don't get why I deleted it. I am not sure if I'll be able to ride until that number, hitting 999.99 miles.

Roman, whom Dima introduced me to, was a stricter vegetarian. They are so-called '"vegan"'.

He had been vegan for 6 years and was a musician.

He released 2 albums on the Internet and made vegan pizza for his part time job. Roman made me a vegan pizza too.

It was without dairy products, eggs and processed meat like ham and sausage. It didn't look tasty, but was quite good.

Instead of meat sausage, soybean sausage and home-made tomato sauce was used.

I was not sure if I was too hungry or if it was really delicious, but it was a different and shocking taste that I had never tried before.

Roman was interested in Korean food culture and he often visited Korean restaurants in Novosibirsk. So I made him 100% vegan Korean food.

I served mushroom rice and soy sauce seasoning.

I was not the only person who Roman allowed to stay in his house. There was a group of travellers; three men and three women.

They were friends travelling around Russia with a very old Lada car. They were really amazing.

They seemed to travel freely and take on new adventures; a. trip to wander freely in a desert, mountains, forest, backcountry or city.

What was interesting were the volleyball nets and volleyballs they had carried with them, a broken trumpet (probably because the car was so old that they carried it to sound their horns when it did not work) and things like recorders.

I imagined that if I hang out with them, I would not feel bored.

Another interesting thing was that they were travelling with sponsors from the company that made the tea they drank.

Not the normal tea bag one. A traditional type of tea.

One time, we went to an open concert in a city and they took photos and videos to shoot not only tea leaves, but also a burner, Koppel, small teapots, traditional ceramic teacups and the moments they brewed and drank the tea sitting on the grass.

Maybe it was because they had to submit them to the sponsored company.

The tea leaves would be left and they allowed me to take some tea leaves if I needed, but I politely refused.

Hello, My Friends in Korea!

I had less than one month left to stay in Russia.

I thought that I should ride hard every day without a break to get out of Russia and take a rest in Kazakhstan within the remaining period.

The temperature difference between morning and evening got very severe.

The lowest temperature in the morning dropped to 7 degrees but it exceeded 25 degrees during the day.

Even when it got cold in the morning and evening, the mosquitoes still existed and they came to bite me. In a place where there were few people, they must have been so excited because after living on the juice from a tree every day, it was an opportunity to taste a different kind of blood which was from Asia.

It's like the same case that a person who eats vegetables every day and someday gets the chance to eat Korean beef sirloin with unlimited refills for free.

From about 6 o'clock getting off the bicycle until the sun went down, or even 10 o'clock, it was their golden time to taste my blood.

So, I thought that I should take a shower as soon as possible and have dinner quickly or in my tent.

As I went out of the tent, the mosquitoes stuck into me but inside of the tent, I was safe. I was invincible.

The ones who entered the tent were what I would easily kill.

Strangely, I could not find any mosquitoes in the late evening or in the morning when the temperature sharply dropped.

Maybe they overslept.

It was really fortunate that the mosquitoes were not as diligent as I was.

I met some nice guests on the road.

(I was the owner of the Siberian two-lane highway.) for Peace run!

I sat on my bicycle to ride and a grey-haired old woman was running with a torch.

I stopped to talk with her and told me that there was a support vehicle 1~1 kilometre ahead.

I did my best to ride and get to the vehicle, put my bicycle there and went back to her and ran with her.

It was the only aid for me to run with her which was ordered from my heart.

Running next to her, not just cheering or financial support. I thought that it would be better to help her. After leaving them, the support vehicle overtook me and went forward.

As I kept riding, the same woman was running before me again. This time, I got off the bicycle to run with her, dragging my bicycle. The moment that we ran together was so happy.

I could help and encourage her in this way.

I should have moved 120 kilometres a day, but it was okay even though I could not move the distance.

After some time, after riding the bicycle in short pants, both knees started to ache.

It could be that my clothing got caught in my knees while riding.

I folded my pants up to my thighs but as I rode, it came loose and came down again. While preparing for my journey, I put on four pants; and one of them was lost in Tulun after I washed it and put it on to dry, and I could not put on the other one.

I thought I needed to take turns wearing the other two. It was getting colder but I had only short pants to wear.

Now, I thought that it was unreasonable to ride 150 kilometres a day. The next day after riding 150 kilometres was a rest day.

I felt severe pain in the knees. Riding 120~130 kilometres would be appropriate.

20 to 30 kilometres might not seem that big of a difference in terms of figures, but in reality, the difference made a huge gap in physical condition.

Even if I drove 120~130 kilometres, when I went into the sleeping bag at night, I felt heat on my knees so I slept with my knees pushing out.

Ah! These days, I got up and had a hot coffee and rolled-cake, listening to the song 'Sigh' by Lee H-I. This was the happiest moment; Thinking that 'I was not the only one who had difficulty.' And getting consolation e and power to ride for the day.

I was in Kurgan.

Before getting here, I stayed in Omsk for 2 days at IIya's house, which Roman introduced me to.

I had planned to just stay for one day but the weather forecast said there would be thunder and lightning the next day, so I stayed one more day.

On the second day, IIya invited me to watch his band perform at the pub.

He was the main vocalist in the rock band, and the atmosphere in the pub that day was very hot, like a concert of a famous rock group.

The crowd threw their clothes off and bumped into each other, and IIya threw himself into the crowd, who carried him and moved him around. It was shocking to see such a concert.

I just stayed away to look at them; did not enjoy it, which made me feel a bit sorry. I stayed for two days in Kurgan through couch-surfing.

I decided to take a rest for two days when I could have the chance to stay in a house. I might need time to charge.

One of the hosts asked me why I had not found a sponsor and rode by myself.

As I prepared and started my journey, I had confidence to get to my final destination, England. But, why did I not find the sponsor?

Because I had confidence to do it by myself, and there was no proof or case to show it. Now, I had moved so far distance, so I would start it.

I was not sure if it could be made. But wish me luck!

I Got Drunk in Ufa

I would describe the weather of Russia from late summer to winter in one word as 'rain'. One day, my friend said this.

"Originally, in Russia, it rained non-stop from mid-August. But this year, there were many sunny days."

"Oh, that was because I was riding in Russia.'" For sure, it was just a joke.

But as God listened to what I had said, there were few sunny days. A cloudy day without rain was a great day for riding.

But, there were few days when the weather was like that. It rained at least once a day.

The drizzle was fine so I could get hit to ride but if it rained heavily, I had to take a rest until the rain stopped.

When I discovered rain clouds in the distance, I prepared in advance and avoided the rain.

Sometimes, the rain clouds moved to another direction which could be a waste of time for me, but it was better to be prepared.

There is a saying, 'Think a thousand times and cut it at one time.' But I want to change it to, 'Ride and ride instead of guessing a thousand times if it would rain or not '

And if it starts to drop, then find a place to avoid it.

I stayed under eaves from the rain for most of the time, but one day, I couldn't find a place to avoid it and stayed under a tree. The leaves were so grateful to me.

Unexpectedly, by couch-surfing, I stayed in Miass, a small town in the middle of the Ural Mountains. To get to the city, I had to get off the main road but was lucky to sleep under a roof.

Alex, the host of the house, allowed me to stay in another house.

His grandmother used to live in the house but passed away a while ago, so he allowed couch-surfers to use the place.

When I went out to the porch, I saw a majestic view of the Ural Mountains.

It was a beautiful landscape that, for a moment, turned into a worried thought, 'Oh, how hard could it be?'

It's a bicycle journey.

In the afternoon, I looked around Miass in the car of Alex's friend. There was a lake, which was called a sister of Baikal.

It was a famous tourist attraction because the water was so clear and clean.

There were also a few yachts on the lake, but the wind was blowing so hard that it didn't look very peaceful.

The next morning, Alex came to the place where I had was staying to make Pelmeni, a traditional Russian dish and snacks.

After some time, he went out to the driving academy and his brother came to the house. With jam and tomato sauce as a present, which was made in their home.

I left Miass with his greeting, and the next city seemed to be famous for its resorts without my intention.

There were so many beautiful sceneries and luxurious houses, so I think like that. "I am in Ufa across the Ural Mountains."

I could stay in a house by Warm Showers.

I could get the house with muddy water splashing on me. It was probably like a mouse drowning in muddy water.

The host told me to take a warm shower in the restroom to care for me. And served me a warm meal.

After relaxing and falling into a nap, I woke up to find a surprise awaiting me – a small evening party.

I couldn't communicate with them naturally but enjoyed the time with many people.

There were lots of different kinds of alcohols like red wine, white wine, tequila, Captain Morgan... I did not hesitate to toast, in order to celebrate that I finally crossed the Ural Mountains.

It was quite difficult to cross the Ural Mountains.

It was cold as the altitude was high and it kept raining, making it difficult to bear the cold.

My hand holding the handle felt like it was breaking, so whenever I bumped into a rest area, I stopped to take a rest in front of a bonfire.

As it was a road that crossed a mountain range, there were countless ups and downs. Of course, the hills were not quite high.

Moreover it was the rain, not the hills, that bothered me.

Because of the rain that did not stop even at night, I slept in my tent in an abandoned truck, and I was yelled at by the owner the next morning.

After crossing the Ural Mountains, it would usually be called Europe in terms of geography. I had wanted to get to Europe, my final destination and goal.

Getting there, I would feel like my dream had come true, which made me not quit and keep going. But the Ural Mountains did not let me go easily, as it was the last gateway to Europe.

Taking a Rest in Kazakhstan

I am in Uralsk which was not included in Russia. I planned to take a rest for a week.

lying in a hotel bed.

I had to ride about 400 kilometres to get here from Ufa via Orenburg. I made a lot of interesting cases.

I could stay in a house in Orenburg.

I was able to arrive earlier than I expected so I visited the bicycle shop to check the brakes on my bicycle. I was fully wet in the rain.

I was worried about the situation in that I might make the shop dirty with the rain dripping down from my body.

Fortunately, the owner didn't care about that and welcomed me and offer the repairing and checking service for bike.

While my bicycle was being repaired, the owner served me warm tea and cake, and I told him about my bicycle journey including stories from Ulan-Ude to here, and my plan to get to England.

He encouraged me as the journey had been tough, and wished me luck.

He repaired my brakes for free and even gave me a tube and brake pads as presents. I had been helped and welcomed by countless people on my way to get here.

They didn't ask for anything from me and just helped, and shared with me who were just young bicycle travellers.

Actually, these were the memories that would not be forgotten for a long time on the trip.

These warm hearts and feelings between people, that were not big but warm, were better than any beautiful sceneries or great civilization or cultures.

How could I count the favour from the bicycle shop owner in terms of money?

While I was travelling through China, Mongolia, and Siberia, I was able to ride bravely with those thoughts and energies.

I stayed overnight at a couch-surfing host's house. The next day, my host needed to visit his grandmother, so I transitioned to a hostel after spending a day there. I found the cheapest hostel in town by searching on the Internet.

After check-in, I asked the host if I could keep my bicycle inside and she asked me if I was a bicycle traveller and provided me one-day for free.

Wow! I was so lucky.

In the afternoon, while wandering the town, I stopped by a small coffee shop to grab a coffee and a doughnut, and the café owner talked to me with curiosity of me being an Asian.

Are you travelling now? Where are you from? How did you get here? Etc…

I showed him the route which I had taken and he was surprised about it, "'Wow. It's unbelievable. Where will you stay today?'"

I told him that I could sleep in a hostel today, for free, thanks to the owner of the hostel.

"'Oh, then this café serves free coffee and doughnuts to bicycle travellers.'"

"'Oh, then can I postpone this chance to tomorrow morning?'"

"'Why not? I'm gonna tell this to the staff who works tomorrow morning.'" I could feel their hearts to give me a present somehow.

Next morning, I visited the café again and the staff gave me a cup of coffee and a doughnut and a small box with encouraging words from the owner.

There were Vietnamese mixed coffee and portable drip coffee.

I drank the coffee in a very special take-out cup that the owner drew a map of Eurasia on, and me riding a bicycle on.

The cup felt like a work of art, too precious to sip from. It seemed wrong to discard it. I felt good for a long time because only good things happened to me.

The wind was blowing from the back, so the bicycle was fast.

On the way to Kazakhstan, people selling yellow melons and watermelons stopped me. And gave one piece of melon.

It was a fruit that I had not tried in Korea, and tasted to have a mixed taste of some kinds of Korean melons. After eating the melon, I checked the map and found that it was in the wrong direction.

I thought that just going south was the direction to Kazakhstan, but it was not right. I should have ridden south-eastward, but rode just south.

I rode for about 50 kilometres for the day but had no choice but to go back... I had no choice but to do it.

If I kept going that way, I would have to ride another 300 kilometres from Kazakhstan, so I would not make it.

When I started riding in the day, the wind blew from the back so I could easily ride, but now that I was going back, I had to overcome the wind with my whole body.

Besides, it started to rain.

It was embarrassing to visit the café again where I had said goodbye in the morning. but when I got to Orenburg, I just thought about going to the café again.

The owner was not in the café but the staff whom I met in the morning was there. The staff served me a cup of warm café coffee and I told the story which I had suffered. And I went to the same hostel where I had stayed the day before.

I felt so embarrassed and sorry for visiting again...

After taking a shower and lying on the bed, the café owner called me to ask if I could visit the café now.

I would express my gratitude and visit the café again. I thanked him so much.

And he unexpectedly asked me if I had a sponsor. Of course, I said no.

He said that he would contact me again after checking to find a sponsor. And he asked me the specific route that I planned.

Do you want to know what happened? The very next day, he contacted me.

A sports shop named 'Trial-Sport' would be the sponsor.

OMG, I couldn't even speak one sentence in Russian but the first sponsor I got was a Russian company.

While taking a rest in Uralsk, I sat in front of my laptop to finish the proposal and opened the lid of sparkling water to drink.

"Oh my god." The sparkling water just ran out and spilled on my laptop. And the keyboard and pad were broken.

I gave up on thinking positively.

Hot tea and cookies that the shop owners gave me for free when I went in for a quick lunch, couch-surfer hosts, a Warm Showers hosts, café owners, bicycle shop owners…

All the people who I happened to meet and who helped me were the sponsors that encouraged me.

Penza Penza Penza After

One person told me that the roads in Kazakhstan were really messy while the highways in Siberia were better than that.

I rode for about 150 kilometres from Russia to Uralsk and I didn't think that it was a complete mess. But the way back to Russia was the worst.

While riding, I was murmuring like this:

"Unpaved roads would be better."

"It would be much better than this to ride on."

"This road could be the worst road in the world."

While riding on the road, I held the handle while moving it, and I felt like my hands were shaking even when I went to bed.

The final camping in Kazakhstan was right in front of the border; to save time to cross the border the next day.

I was worried about the situation that the armies or policemen might keep me sleeping there because it was a border area, but they didn't care about it.

They sat in for the whole night, providing an escort, and I could sleep without any worries.

Jerome, a French man I met in Mongolia, had to stay for 3 days on the border because of a visa issue in Middle Asian countries. It brings back memories of that night…

I didn't spend as much time as I expected and had 2 more hours.

The two countries were so close but they had a time difference of two hours. It was a strange experience.

On the day I crossed the border around 3 pm, I wanted to drink a cup of hot tea and stopped at a rest stop next to a gas station.

I parked my bicycle to order a cup of tea and some snacks.

The owner looked at my bicycle parked out, let the staff make pasta and told me to sleep here if I had not decided where I would sleep.

I was totally grateful.

After sleeping one night outside, the next day I should sleep in a house to relax. I was not the only person who the owner favoured.

Mongolia Rally travellers, motorcyclists….

When the travellers charged the gas at the gas station right next to his place, he invited them to his place and let me see their photos.

I got off the bicycle at 3 o'clock and experienced Russian culture.

I soaked myself in a Russian-style sauna in his house, named 'banya', and in the evening ate 'shashlik', which was grilled over charcoal for a long time.

I also drank 'samogon', a homemade Russian liquor and he fired on it saying that good samogon fired on it.

I could not stop just showing the show, so I should drink it.

It was much better than the vodka sold in the market and the flavour was so clean. I was able to experience Russian culture in half a day.

I want to tell you a story about the Russian police.

All people who travelled in cars or motorcycles hated Russian police. They loved money.

It was said that the traffic cops particularly made much more money from traffic fines than their salaries.

Traffic police hid in the forest and checked the speed with a camera, or looked at a car coming from a far with a telescope. If the drivers were putting on their seat belts, they fined the drivers.

When riding, I could easily see this situation. There were even worse cases.

It was also said that the traffic cops would put fines or get money after checking that the drivers were foreigners, even when they drove under the speed limit.

It was fortunate that the targets for Russian police were just for vehicles, and I had never experienced friction with the ones I met on the road.

Rather, they gave me a thumbs up.

Once, I had friction with a cop in Saratov.

I was wandering before a cell phone shop to contact the Warm Showers host.

I was in short pants, and slippers soaked in the rain, and a cop passing by approached me to see my passport.

I didn't want to unpack my luggage in the rain so I let him see my passport photo on my phone. The cop took me to the police station because he didn't like my attitude. Realising that it would make the situation worse, I showed him my passport and Korea-Russia Mutual Agreement in Russian, which I always carried, and told him that I was on a bicycle tour.

Also, I showed him the map showing my journey. After that, his attitude totally changed.

He shook his hands, patted my back and even took photos with me. In short, the Russian police were all good people to me.

Worst case.

A few days before, the right pedal made a bad sound and then suddenly fell out. I should ride another 70 kilometres to get to Penza, the big city there.

I could hardly ride the bicycle without one side pedal with my slippers on.

I had to step deeper on the right pedal to turn the pedal because it was out of balance. Penza was a city surrounded by mountains.

Could you imagine?

It was difficult to explain how hard it would be, because I had used the word 'hard' too much. I just continued to swear and get to Penza, crying all the way.

I visited my sponsor company 'Trial-Sport,' and they repaired my pedal for free, put a sticker on the pannier so that anyone could see that it was the sponsors, and then gave me a hoodie with the words Trial-Sport on it.

Once again, I wanted to express my gratitude to the café owner.

Jumping from the Sky in Russia.

The Warm Showers host gave me a helmet as a present.

A friend who lived in St. Petersburg put it on the host's house before moving in.

If the helmet didn't fit on me, he said that when I arrived in St. Petersburg, I could return it to the original owner.

Killing two birds with one stone.

Getting a helmet and a chance to get a place to stay in St. Petersburg. When I put on the helmet, I felt confident to look like a biker.

But as I put on the helmet, I took it off after exactly 3 hours.

It was the first time in my life that I put on a helmet, so it was too painful for the muscles in the back of my neck to keep it on.

I tried to pretend to be a bicycle rider but had pain in my neck, and luggage to take to St. Petersburg to deliver.

I thought that it was best for me to just ride freely.

It is autumn in Russia now.

The leaves changed their clothes, or fell off one by one and lay quietly on the road; even I did not see that the rice got yellow and bowed or the sky so blue.

I am a man and felt restless in autumn!

On the road to Moscow, once I found a hostel on the main road, I just rode to stay for a one-day riding destination.

I visited hotels occasionally when necessary. I opted for ones near the main route I was riding, ensuring affordability. Most of these hotels were placed near the villages.

But this was unusual because there were always small villages near the hotel, but I couldn't see any villages in this place.

But it was better because it was not far from the main street.

Arriving at the hotel, there were buildings like pensions built in the wild field. I intuitively thought, 'oh, this must be really expensive for me to stay.'

But I asked and the cheapest dormitory room was 700 roubles.

The owner spoke English very well and I decided to stay for a day with the expectation to communicate with them in a while.

The owner invited me to the staff party at the restaurant in the evening.

I was sitting uncomfortably at the party and one person of my age came to me with an interest in bicycle travelling and introduced this place to me.

This was like a base camp for skydivers.

Every weekend, members or people who want to learn come here and stay for the weekend. He offered me to try skydiving while I was here, but the price was 8,000 roubles.

The next day, the weather was so nice that I decided to go skydiving and stay one more day. Skydiving was one of the things on my bucket lists, so I was on the plane in my friend's arms with expectation. With the door opening, the plane kept soaring into the sky.

It went up until the base camp looked like a little dot that could not be recognised.

I wondered how I could jump out of here to the base camp because it was so high.

Finally, the captain allowed me to jump off with a signal, and I fell to the ground while hugging my friend.

He said that he would make me feel more interested and showed his skills; turning forward and backward in the air and rotating on both sides.

When we got closer to the earth, he unfolded the paraglider and shouted, turning the direction in a hurry.

"Isn't it really fun?"

I could not say anything.

I just murmured to myself after safely landing on base camp where I could not see toward the sky.

"Oh, I'm alive."

Actually, as I got on the plane and went up, the air pressure changed rapidly and I felt pain in my ears.

But when I came down, it hurt more than when I went up to the sky.

Also, because of my excited friend, I actually had a little motion sickness.

I was sitting on the grass and drinking a hot tea to take a rest, when he came to me to offer more diving.

"'Oh, no, thank you.'"

I did skydive, took photos and rode longboards with them. Getting to Moscow a day later didn't make big changes.

The weather was so nice that I needed to lie down on the grass and take a rest. All the people who worked here were very excited.

They did their work during the week and came here on weekends to teach students how to skydive and enjoy doing it.

They were always excited; maybe because of skydiving too much. I just spent one day together but I could get close with them.

I thought that there would be a density in time after meeting them.

The Red Square in Moscow

I had a jinx of getting rained on every time I entered a big city, and this worked out when I entered Moscow.

3~4 days before I arrived in Moscow, the weather was very fine, but as I tried to enter Moscow, the sky got dark and it started drizzling.

The street to Moscow was not a highway but a 6-laned road and so many cars were stuck and stopped on the wide roads.

Do you remember Kim Han? We crossed paths near Lake Baikal. We stayed in touch as I trailed behind his faster pace, we planned to reunite in Moscow. I met Han again at the Red Square.

I used to ride on the side road while glancing at the driver's in the cars that were stopped on the roads.

I felt like I was getting revenge for the cars that ran on the open roads.

I met Han again at the Red Square.

Han introduced me to Dong-geun and Dong-woo, who had been crossing Eurasia on motorcycles like Han.

Their motorcycles were awesome. Oh, I thought that I would be happy no matter how cold it was if I could have travelled on such a nice motorcycle.

I stayed in Moscow for 7 days, and 5 days among those, I spent with these Koreans.

We were all travellers and had a lot in common, so it was so comfortable to stay together, and we could communicate in Korean which was best for me.

We shopped at a supermarket with reasonable prices, made Korean dishes at a hostel and bought travel equipment and winter supplies to prepare for the upcoming winter.

What I bought this time was Heattech pants that I had really needed. I met not just Koreans, but also two Russians and a German in Moscow.

When I arrived at Baikal for the first time, someone invited me to their home and let me know their son's phone number, to stay when I would get to Moscow in his house. And his name was Ayur.

It was our first meeting, but we were comfortable as if we knew each other, maybe I had met their family earlier.

Another person, Anton, a vegetarian whom I met in Baikal for the summer vacation, brought me to a vegan restaurant and we had a very healthy meal together.

The staffs wore t-shirts with a logo printed, 'Health is the new sexy' and I could easily see this logo on the wall of the restaurant.

It was so attractive and I can't forget it until now.

As if we hadn't met a close friend in a long time, we greeted each other and had a pleasant conversation.

I'd like to share a shot, amusing anecdote. I met a German girl named Julia.

She came to St. Petersburg as an exchange student, and came to Moscow for about three weeks as an intern before returning home.

We met in a hostel and she could speak Korean with an awkward pronunciation, saying that her close Korean friend taught her Korean.

With an outgoing personality, I could easily notice her as a good person.

We added each other as friends on Facebook and exchanged phone numbers.

I promised to contact her when I got to Germany and passed by the city where Julia lived.

The next day, I moved to another hostel where Korean friends had stayed. Somehow, I had a strong desire to meet her. You know that feeling, right? a message via SMS to Julia and she replied in German, asking who I was.

I told her, "June, who you met at the hostel yesterday," and she replied in German again.

I thought that she was making fun of me so I asked her to be able to reply in English, but she answered that she could not speak in English.

I asked my German friend for help ;To translate 'I am June, who you met in the hostel in Moscow yesterday. I want to meet you tonight. Are you available?' in German.

And I sent what was translated to Julia. Julia read but no answer.

I decided to visit the hostel, hoping that luck might be on my side and I ran to the hostel where I had stayed yesterday and asked the counter staff to ask a favour.

"I have to find a woman from Germany named Julia. She checked in yesterday and would check out tomorrow, and if she comes into the hostel, please give her my number."

As I was coming back to the hostel, I realised that we added each other as friends on Facebook. I sent a message on Facebook and she replied.

I asked her to meet at dinner but she had a meeting for dinner with her friends so after having dinner, she could meet me.

After meeting her, I let her see the message I had sent and asked if the phone number was right. After reading the message, she laughed.

"Oh, sorry. I entered the wrong number."

I had contacted someone I didn't know at all. Having sent a reply, she might be Julia too.

I visited two football teams in Moscow. CSKA Moscow and Spartan Moscow.

The real purpose of my journey was to visit the football training centre and meet coaches to show my passion for football and ask for some advice.

Now, I got to start this which made me so happy.

I thought the coach, staffs and players would welcome me if I rode a bicycle to the training centre and said 'I had ridden here to learn football teaching.' But I was naïve. I have to invest in another time to meet them.

At CSKA Moscow, after enduring five hours in the cold weather, I finally had the chance to meet and converse with the head coach. The coach extended an invitation for me to observe their training session. He also gave me words of encouragement, affirming that I could make an impact even if not as a player.

I reflected on my journey from Korea to Moscow on a bicycle, all for the opportunity to meet the coach and receive a motivational boost right at the training centre.

And the place I went to visit the Spartan Moscow was not 1st training centre but youth training centre. I couldn't talk to anyone there.

I just looked at young children playing football happily for over an hour.

The Last City of Russia, St. Petersburg

As I was shivering in the cold, I came to St. Petersburg quickly so hard.

From Moscow to St. Petersburg, I used Warm Showers twice and couch-surfing once.

Was it great luck to succeed three times while riding only 700 kilometres, compared to couch-surfing and Warm Showers seven times during the thousands of kilometres of journey to Moscow?

Anyway, that was a lot of time.

I could feel that I was in Europe now, to see IKEA and other global brands that I sometimes saw unlike when I was riding in Siberia.

On the way to St. Petersburg, I met two Koreans travelling by car. They ran a tea company in China.

They were travelling to promote traditional tea which they had made.

They planned to pass through Siberia to Europe, entering St. Petersburg and stopped their car to see a Korean bicycle traveller riding with the Korean flag on the road.

They said they could get me on their car to St. Petersburg as I was struggling in cold weather on their car too. But I had declared to myself and promised to visit the Warm Showers host's house so declined politely.

Just in case, I asked if I could get a thick sleeping bag for sleeping in the night and they gave one, explaining that they had kept a spare one but it started losing its inner hair and they decided to throw it.

It was bulky but I was grateful to be able to sleep warmly. They also gave me 2,000 roubles cheering me up to buy a meal.

I used to spend 300 roubles a day while passing through Siberia and it was a lot of money for me. I wanted to thank them again.

I went into an abandoned house to sleep, for the same reason I had slept in an abandoned car when I crossed the Ural Mountains.

It was drizzling on that day, soaking my body and the weather forecast said it would rain the next day as well.

Motels on the road sides offered ridiculously high prices and it was hard to even find such motels. After finishing the distance I had to ride for a day, at around 6 pm, I looked around to find if there was any suitable tree to set up a tent in the rain, and found an abandoned house with an open door.

There was another house next to the abandoned house, and when I found it, the owner of the house came out.

No matter how abandoned the house was, I thought that I should not go in without permission, so I asked the owner of the next house if it was okay for me to stay a night in the abandoned house.

He led me to the abandoned house with a gesture of "'Why not?'"

Then he opened the door of the living room, went into inside and let me sleep where I want to sleep.

It was the first time I went into an abandoned house, but I thought that it would be better to stay outside because of the smell of an empty house, rather than being scared.

Eventually, I decided to set up the tent under the eaves. What I saw then, was an old mattress!

I thought that I could sleep on a really fluffy mat instead of an air mat, so I laid out the mattress and set up my tent on it and could sleep so well.

I slept under the eaves to avoid the rain but the inside of the tent got wet because of dew condensation.

I thought I couldn't stop drying the tent in the morning.

I stayed at the host's house for a week in St. Petersburg. I didn't mean to stay so long, but it just happened.

I spent time shopping with friends, playing football , riding at night, walking around the park, going to a café, visiting a football club training centre or just chilling out at home and thinking about the roads where I had been on.

Just like a local who lived in St. Petersburg for a long time, I spent a week with the daily life of the city.

90 Days and 7,500 Kilometres in Russia

If you had been in the army, you would know.

As you went through all kinds of things together making negative and positive relationships with your colleagues, you could make a sense of friendship.

A negative case would turn into a positive memory and sometimes you might miss that time.

I also had memories from three months of cycling across Russia, and there were some memories that were happy and some that I wanted to forget.

But now that I was leaving Russia, I was just as sad as I had been when I finished serving in the army.

When I spilled out my plan to cross Siberia and Russia by bicycle, my friends were worried about me.

"Why? If you took the Trans-Siberian Railway, you could get to Moscow in three or four days, and you would go by bicycle? Why don't you save your time and travel to Northern Europe where you wanted to go when the weather would be better?"

Russia did not have good road conditions and it would be dangerous because of so many trucks. Even my Russian friends said that they didn't decide to ride on a bicycle road in Russia.

In short, nobody had a positive viewpoint for me to cross Russia by riding. That was true.

The roads in Russia were not as good as I thought.

Some sections were in good condition after the pavement work had been completed but most of other sections were not in good condition, or were unpaved roads; so when I passed, the soil dust was up.

Of course, there were tons of trucks passing by.

Some thoughtful drivers took care of the bicycle travellers, driving slowly and avoided them, but most truck drivers would pass by me so quickly without a care.

There were some cases when trucks passed by me so quickly and made me stumble and dangerous.

Russia was the place where I had stayed for the longest time whether it was good or bad.

That's why it was a place where I had so many stories to share that I liked.

As I was slowly riding and travelling, I could meet a lot of good friends and learned a lot about great places.

I had been helped by so many Russian friends and felt grateful to them. They were the ones who welcomed me so kindly and warmly.

Everyone had prevented me from travelling to Russia by riding, but I ended up crossing Russia thanks to them.

I miss them while I am writing this.

The word I heard the most in Russia: Давай (Davai)!

Bike Tour Tips in Russia

Korea-Russia Mutual Agreement Treaty

South Korea and Russia have signed an agreement since 2014 that allows them to travel in both countries without a visa for 90 days out of 180 days.

But, when first visiting Russia, a person can stay for 60 days, and when staying for 60 days, he or she needs to leave Russia and come back for another 30 days.

Sometimes, police or border checkpoint staffs in Russia don't know this agreement, so just in case, print out the treaty in Russian.

Residence Registration

Within three days after entering Russia, the person should register residence at a hostel or other accommodation.

But bicycle travellers like me could not register their specific residence because they moved around every time or camped somewhere.

One day, a police officer asked me to show my residential registration card and I showed him the map I had ridden for the journey and explained I used to sleep in my tent and he understood me.

Mr Truck

The biggest enemies of riding a bicycle on the Siberian road were trucks. When trucks passed by me, my bicycle used to move from the wind.

But, when I took a rest, they were not the same.

On the roads, there was a place where truck drivers could rest on one side and whoever took a rest used to invite me to give me something to eat like tea, coffee, cookies, and sausages.

It was very cold after fall so it was not good to take a rest outside. It was just a pause.

But after being invited by truck drivers, I got the power to ride again.

To Use Accommodation Facilities at Train Stations

If it rains and the hostel is too expensive, visit a train station in a nearby city.

If it is not too small a station, there would be accommodation facilities where you can rest for a while.

They are reasonably priced and there are four beds in the room and toilet facilities for washing like a guest house.

Customers are mainly travellers for the early morning train, and staffs let them wake up for train time.

Individual towels are also provided separately.

Rain Jacket

Rain jacket is an essential item when passing through Russia. It is not only waterproof but also has a thermal effect.

In autumn when it starts to rain and the temperature drops sharply, it is a must-have item.

Three Baltic Countries Buried in Heavy Snow

Estonia

One Russian friend showed me a picture.

If I visit Estonia, I would be able to see the wonderful view at the border. It was such an amazing view.

In the morning of the final day that I left Russia, with the expectation of moving to other countries, Russia showed me snow as a farewell present.

I slept so well on the loose haired sleeping bag that I had gotten for a present, and woke up to see the world made white by heavy snow.

The tent and bicycle laid in the forest filled with snow. It was such a romantic morning.

But after reflecting on the romantic view for just 10 minutes, I got into the severe situation.

The snowflakes were getting bigger and bigger and I had to get out of Russia as quickly as possible before getting stuck in the snow.

When I got to the border, that is, the same place with the picture Russian friends showed me, the scenery full of snow was truly enchanting.

The word that it's like a picture is stale.

The borders of Russia and Estonia face each other along a river and it looked like they had defended their country with castles built on both sides of the river

Snow, river and old castles, I crossed the border so fast.

After I finally came to my senses, the air in the rear wheel was all gone.

I couldn't change the tube on the snowy road, so I found one bike-shop to and asked the owner if I could change the tube and it was so helpful for me.

What I really felt sorry about was that the molten snow fell from me, my bicycle and the luggage which made the floor of the shop dirty.

I tried to clean the floor by myself, but the owner stopped me, saying, "You don't have to. It's okay," and even gave me a tube as a gift.

While I changed the tube, the snow didn't stop and even kept piling up.

On the day all that I had to do was cross the border, but I felt that I should bike a little more and get to the next city.

It was about 10 kilometres from the border city, Narva.

The snowy road was slippery, it was cold but somehow, I endured it and kept pedalling and a car passed by me pouring melted water on me.

As I endured and kept pedalling, my feeling was completely turned upside down and I didn't want to ride the bicycle anymore.

When I lost control, the cold I had endured became much more unbearable, and I lost the reason why I should keep going down this slippery road with the cold.

I turned the direction to Narva, where I left.

And I entered a hotel and soaked myself in a warm water tube. My body melted and also my feeling got better.

It was still snowing the next morning.

I wrapped my feet with a plastic bag and put on shoes to prevent the severe wind from entering my shoes.

At first, I was quite satisfied with the effect of the plastic bags, but the effect didn't last for more than half a day.

I felt freezing cold like my hands and feet would break, so I stopped many times to exercise to make my hands and feet warmer.

Suddenly, I wondered 'what have I done?'

I believed to get to Europe if I would pedal every day even if the ride to Europe was far. Despite the cold of Siberia, I thought that Europe would be fine.

Every travelling before leaving looks awesome.

When I had left my country, other people had said that I'm crazy and tried to stop me. So I believed that if I did and finished this travel, my passion would be recognised and it would become a driving force to move forward to my dream.

With the expectation that if I visit the club training centre from Korea to Europe by riding a bicycle, the directors of the club would be willing to meet me and I could get advice that can make my dream for football realised from them.

But I realised that the gap between my dream and reality was so big.

It is hard for me to meet the director but getting an opportunity to talk to them was even harder.

I figured out that travelling by riding a bicycle was just that, and to realise my dream for football I should invest in it separately.

Although, crossing Eurasia by riding a bicycle, I got so passionate that I could be willing to try for any challenge and lesson of life that I should get an aim and keep trying.

From whom in the world can I learn a better lesson than this?

So, even if I was discouraged for a moment as my condition and mind was gone, I couldn't settle down.

I stayed in Tallinn with Dong-geun running around Old Town and the castle and travelling for 3 days.

Running on the streets of Old Town not filled with tourists who didn't start their day with a calm mood was a novel way to enjoy this city.

I could feel the real attraction of this city running in the morning.

And in the afternoon, I walked to some places that I had run and felt nice again, took some pictures and sat enjoying the leisure moments.

Before I left this city, I met one person while running. Bicycle traveller, a colleague from the same planet.

We had the same direction to leave and he had planned to leave today.

He said that he had gotten Warm Showers host for 3 days and if I came there, I would be able to ride together.

I decided to meet him again and ride together. I was not going to ride in the cold alone.

Latvia

When I moved from Estonia to Latvia, I rode on a village road instead of the main road used by a lot of cars.

I liked this village road even if it was a little more time-consuming road and not a paved one.

It was because I could feel that I'd done a real trip as I rode on the village road while breathing in the fresh air, rather than on a road where big trucks spit smoke and run by me.

Would I say that I finally got to know the attraction of riding?

As I was riding off the main road, sometimes unowned apple trees with their fruits were standing. When I saw them, I stopped, picked some apples for a bite, and put some in my bag.

Apples just picked from the tree have a crunchy texture and taste so fresh.

It is half the size of an apple we see in the supermarket, but twice as sweet, so I think it tastes like honey.

The weird thing was that after eating the apple, I felt so well digested. As soon as I ate it, I went to the toilet directly.

I experienced Halloween culture for the first time in Latvia.

I bought a chocolate box to give to a host connected by couch-surfing. I had no idea that day was Halloween.

The house of the host was completely in the rural section, and there were no other houses nearby.

In the evening, the hostess said that last Halloween, children living in the village came to get some candy but she didn't know what it would be like this year.

It was when the host couple and I were enjoying Halloween. Car lights came through the dark window....

The hostess turned off the lights and lit candles.

She took some chocolate that I gave to her, and put them in a small box, waiting for the children to arrive.

Two girls who appeared to be sisters, dressed up for Halloween to get candy and chocolate. The hostess gave them a box of chocolates.

The girls looked at me, with their appearance showing that they waited for another gift.

The hostess said to them that I didn't prepare some candy and they sprinkled me with flour. I was sprinkled with flour without knowing the reason.

I didn't prepare not only candy but also to be sprinkled with flour, which didn't make me feel good. I didn't feel good, but it was their culture, what can I do?

Anyway, I could experience Halloween culture and also get sprinkled with flour in another country. Next morning, I took a picture with the host's family and left the house.

But, the dog from the host's house was chasing after me as I left the road.

Well, I just thought that he was gonna see me off the village and didn't pay attention to him that much, but the dog continued to follow me even though I passed through the village and entered the main road.

I must be about 15 kilometres away for the dog to stop and follow me again.

At first, he was full of energy as much as he was followed by me going ahead and behind me, but after a few minutes, he must have felt too exhausted to keep running.

I couldn't just let him alone and leave.

Because I thought that if I left him, he could go back to the host's house alone.

I had no choice but to feed the dog some water and follow the dog's pace while riding slowly. It was impossible to take the dog anymore.

I decided to call the phone number written on the dog's collar and let them know this. I entered a shop to buy some bread and borrow a phone to make a call.

It was easy to buy some bread because I was paying for it.

But I had difficulty in asking for favour to borrow the phone even though I tried to say it.

I had no choice but to get out of the shop and then, I heard a horn from behind. It was the host's car. The host took the dog in the car as if it wasn't a big deal, saying that the dog often followed the guests. And I felt a little disappointed at the same time.

I felt like I could write a wonderful travelling story with a dog.

Obviously, I was so glad that the dog was able to find his owner.

I don't remember anything but "snow" in Latvia.

I was able to meet the Australian friend who I met in Tallinn again at a Warm Showers host's house, and he was very excited about the snow.

It was the first time he had seen this heavy snow falling from the sky and I could understand him. Something weird, pretty and attractive is all unfamiliar.

He felt so happy.

He pressed the shutter of his smart phone countless times.

It was the first time for him to see snow but he rode to enter this snow-covered world which must have felt so ecstatic and refreshing.

But that was just until then.

After a few hours, he mumbled "Shit, please, stop this snow!" with swearing.

I guess he must have remembered that snow was a disaster from the sky. As the snow piled up, everything got problematic.

I slipped and fell on the road; my hands and feet were so cold, and I couldn't drink water that I had brought because of the freezing wind.

Later, I could moisten my throat that felt like tearing while eating candy that I bought.

Happily, I discovered a more effective solution for the problem of holes forming in the plastic bags I had wrapped around my feet.

I wrapped my feet tightly with plastic wrap like wrapping pig's feet in warp at a butcher's store, which prevented my socks from getting wet and gave much better effective cold protection than just putting on a plastic bag.

It was literally evolution. I think there is a reason humans have survived not to be extinct. I survived even on snow-covered roads and still pedalled toward England.

Lithuania

Lithuania was similar to Estonia and Latvia. It always snowed. But it was fortunate that I was not alone this time but together.

Whenever a strong headwind blew, we took turns relying on each other by pedalling to block the wind in front of us.

Accompany. the Australian friend who got tired of the snow and cold, suggested to take a bus from Riga to Poland.

But I insisted on riding.

He followed my suggestion and gave up getting on the bus which made us suffer more because of me.

As was common during winter, Warm Showers hosts usually respond positively to our requests. This held true even in Lithuania. A Warm Showers host came to our rescue, extending an invitation that included a comfortable bed and a warm dinner.

What I liked the most was the heart of the host; with a warm heart rather than a warm bed.

The host couple looked to be of similar age as my parents or a little older, and they made me feel as if I was at home in Korea.

They had experience in helping bicycle travellers before we stayed.

I guess the travellers had also felt like family, the way I felt. On one side of the living room door, we could see a bunch of postcards from them hanging on the door.

I wanted to give something to them too, so we took a picture together with a Polaroid and gave it to them as a present.

It was not only expression of their favour, but also hope to remember the time we shared together.

In Lithuania, I had tried 'shakotis', a traditional snack of Lithuania, although I didn't try traditional food in Estonia and Latvia.

It looked a little eccentric, like being angry.

It looked like that but was so sweet and soft, because it was made with egg yolk as the main ingredient. Some cookies had chocolate on the tip which was much better than nothing.

The recipe was very unique.

It was baked, rotating it over fire like a whole pig barbecue, and when the dough was properly cooked, the dough was put on top of it to make it in layers.

I think it was only in Lithuania.

If you have a chance to visit Lithuania, you should try this.

When planning the trip, the three Baltic countries were one of the places I had wanted to visit. After leaving the three Baltic countries, 'snow' was the only thing that I remembered.

I wanted to escape from the snow and clouds so I tried to ride to the south where it was warmer, so I felt pity that I couldn't really feel about these countries.

Will I ever get another chance to ride a bike in the summer when it will be snow free? Just because you want it doesn't mean you can get it all.

But if you don't give up on your dream, won't the day that you get it come some day? I had no choice but to keep the three Baltic countries on my dream list.

Bike Tour Tips in Three Baltic Countries

How to Get Extra Tubes

During the bicycle trip, I changed my tube 12 times or more. After it snowed, I needed to change the tube in a bicycle shop. Because it was too cold to change it outside, every time I changed the flat tube with my extra one. The owners of the shops gave me another tube as a gift to encourage me.

If you want to get extra tube in cold weather, put on shabby clothes for doing a bicycle trip. Then every owner would give you some.

How to Protect from the Cold – Needless to Say

You must buy thick ski gloves for your hands, and wrap your feet as much as possible. You must put on heat-tech for top and bottom and over it, one more athletic tights.

The Baltic in October is really cold.

You must wear enough to think you can live with it.

Stay Indoors to Take Enough Rest

For sure once you enter a café, you need to order at least one food or a cup of beverage at least. So I didn't enter a café to save my money.

Going to the supermarket was better.

I could buy some groceries, didn't need to care for other people and could relax in a warm space. While riding a bicycle, I felt like my hands and feet were going to.

I rested more often than in Russia.

Not to get frostbite, whenever you took a time for break, you need to exercise or clap your hands to make better blood circulation.

Do Not Buy SIM Card

The mileage for all three countries is less than 400 kilometres.

If you start a riding trip, search for couch-surfing, Warm Showers or some other accommodation like a hostel, and you do not need to buy SIM card for travelling the three countries.

Good Bye Snow, Poland

Unstoppable Pedal

It was very nice weather when I went to Poland.

The sky was clear, the sun was warm, the country road of Poland was peaceful, so I could talk a lot with my Australian friend without any concern.

When we arrived at the Air bnb I made a reservation at, the host was out of the house.

We had no choice but to wander the village and happened to get to know one person who lived in the city. He invited us to serve warm soup and bread made by his mother.
They were so kind. They offered us to stay in their house.

The son went a step further by scheduling an appointment with a bike shop to repair my long-troubled bicycle.

When going uphill, the pedals often rattled and clicked, and my friend from Australia recommended that I change the chin and sprockets.

It is said that the chain stretches and does not match well with sprockets after riding about 3,000 to 4,000 kilometres.

So bicycle manufacturers usually recommend changing the chain when getting to that level. But I didn't know that and kept riding, which caused this problem.

It had been through hot summer and cold snowy weather, so the chain was stretched and when I put a little force to the pedal, it would spin in vain.

I had some pain and even thought that I could die if I continued riding like this. It was just about 80 kilometres from Augustów to Białystok.

After changing the chain and sprocket, the bike worked much better than before, but the weather got bad again and the highest temperature was around 4 degrees. After lunch, it started to snow and my whole body got wet, and my hands were too frozen to move my fingers.

To hold the brakes, I needed to move my shoulder back, and my feet were worse than my hands. The snow on the front wheel splashed, which made my shoes wet.

Furthermore, snow accumulated from the front wheel jammed the gear mechanism, preventing me from shifting into 1st and 3rd gears, except for the 2nd gear.

But I couldn't stop riding. If I had stopped riding, it would have felt like my heart stopped.

I entered the centre of the city without a destination, to enter a department store without keeping my bicycle carefully. But as I inhaled the warm air, I could not breathe as there was a heavy pain in my lungs.

My body was in such bad condition. I felt like falling down if something went a little bit wrong. The Australian friend was also lost. He threw his gloves and cursed.

Luckily, we could get to contact a Warm Showers host and she allowed us to come now if we were near.

We barely got to the house, enduring the cold, and the host opened the door and went out. We squatted before the heater to warm ourselves and saved our lives.

I cannot forget the pain I had at that time.

Can you even imagine how much worse this feels? Picture your body freezing in the bitter cold, then finally warming up under a hot shower. Now, multiply that discomfort by a hundred.

After suffering this cold, I realised that I could not keep riding in this way, so I decided to go by train to Warsaw.

Warsaw was very sunny and it never snowed.

The period was Independence Day holiday, so the whole city looked busy preparing for the event.

Warm Showers host went back to her home town to meet her family, so I needed to take care of the house and spent time going to the café nearby.

On my first visit, I guess I looked like an outsider from the East, 'cause a bunch of kids who seemed like they were in elementary school came up to chat and hang out.

And they told me, "Smoke! Smoke!" and I shook my head and they went out to smoke. Wow.... I felt they were young.

After leaving Warsaw, I could keep staying in host's houses to be allowed by Warm Showers.

Hosts allowed me to stay in their house so kindly and they were interested in my trip.

The benefits of staying with Warm Shower's hosts;

First of all, the hosts love riding and most of them have experience of riding trips, even though it's short.

And they also have experience of using Warm Showers so they understand the guest's situations and feelings.

What riding travellers need after the day riding;

To take a shower with warm water.

To eat food to stop the hunger.

To sleep in a cosy bed to complement our condition. These are enough.

During dinner time, we talk a lot to share trip stories because we have a common point, riding trip. But, don't spend too much time on that.

Hosts have to work on the next day, and travellers should also prepare for tomorrow.

Łódź is a city that is 100 kilometres from Warsaw.

A host that I met in Łódź was Philip, who was my age.

He still lived with his parents, and was an MTB bike player in his teenagers and worked in a bike company.

There was a park with thick trees in front of their house and a wall heater to make their house warm in the living room.

There were lots of plants in the dining room and I was able to look at the park behind the window of the dining room; that was an amazing house.

Philip's father, who had retired, would make some nice dishes, and I could not forget the taste of the Polish pancake. Putting ricotta cheese on a thin pancake, rolling it up and biting it, it was so yummy. It is eaten for breakfast but I ate so many pieces and did not stop eating even till lunch time.

Another memorable dish is vegan burger.

Generally, vegan burgers have a soybean patty, but some unique person had made a pumpkin patty. Pumpkin patty, cheese, basic vegetables for classic burgers, and a few pomegranates. Once I took a bite of it, I felt like getting healthy.

The pumpkin patty was so good, much better than I expected.

If I travel to Poland again, then I would visit Łódź to eat the vegan burger again.

I bought my luggage carrier to get rid of the old one which was totally broken, and Philip took me to his office so as to repair my bike.

I did not feel any trouble with it but the expert viewed it as dangerous.

He repaired the pedals to work better, replaced some parts and adjusted the spokes again.

Wrocław felt old-fashioned, unlike Warsaw.

In the Old Town it felt like a long time, the Christmas market had been opened from the week I arrived and there were many items that showed the Christmas atmosphere, and crafts to enjoy and buy. The most common booth was selling warm Christmas wine.

I tired tried drinking Christmas wine for the first time; it had a strong cherry scent. In the cold winter, it was so good to drink it looking around the Old Town.

Some dwarfs that we could see in a fairy tale named Snow White were there, and they rolled a little ball on the corner of the street or took a rest sitting on the window sill.

But if you just focus on looking around the big buildings, then you would not recognise. So take it slow and pay attention to them.

Bike Tour Tips in Poland

Sim Card

Poland is a member of the EU but they use the Polish currency and the price is very cheap. Especially, the SIM card was especially cheap.

If you buy one for 10GB with 4G speed here, then you need to pay around 10 Euros. I had so much data left that I rode with video call on.

Lantern

When you ride in Poland, you must have a lantern on the front and the back. It was the first country that had legal policy for it out of all my whole riding trips. Of course, even if it was not pushed by law, the lantern is necessary for safety.

Thankfully, there was no country where helmets were mandatory for the riders to wear for riding trips.

Czech Republic as Beautiful As Switzerland

In Serene Prague

It was 350 kilometres to ride through the Czech Republic. At my regular cycling pace, I could have breezed through it in 4 days. But things didn't quite go as planned. I ended up spending 10 days in the Czech Republic, and out of those, I only managed to ride for 3 days.

As I moved from Poland to the Czech Republic, I could have a wonderful scenery like Switzerland before me.

I had never been to Switzerland but often looked at the scenery in photos so I could guess they were similar.

Sheep grazing on mountains and wide pastures, narrow canyons and two-lane roads between them. The way from Prague to Pilsen had nice natural scenery which was very attractive.

One time, I took a detour down a side road to check out some natural beauty and guess what? I ended up totally lost. Not a great experience.

I'm a fan of cruising down those quiet country roads, so I kept hugging the edge more and more. Then I saw a sign that said this road could take me across a river. I figured there might be a bridge or something similar. With that in mind, I pedalled on, hoping to cross the river and make my way to my destination for the day.

However, upon reaching the designated spot, I was met with a surprise. There was no bridge in sight, but I did spot small ferry boats moored on either side of the river.

The boatman was nowhere to be seen and just the ferry boats were there.

As I went back to the road which I had passed, I could not see anything in front of me without turning the lantern on because the sun had set.

Sadly, the lantern did not last more than 10 minutes and then it was gone.

I had no choice but to ride holding my smart phone for a little light on the dark road.

I rode to my destination concentrating on riding for safety, and I realised that Korea is so awesome to have lots of streetlights standing every 100 metres everywhere.

When there was a light, a small stone was no problem which turned into a big hazard if the light disappeared.

I should concentrate much more and be careful.

The biggest lesson from this experience was to finish riding before the sunset!

I stayed in Prague for a week and for 4 days, during which I ran looking around Old Town in the morning.

Prague is a famous city crowded by tourists from all over the world.

Except for at dawn, all of downtown is crowded with many tourists, so if someone tours, he could watch many tourists at the tourism spots.

But in the early morning, if you run from a hostel which is located near Prague Central Station to Prague Castle, you can enjoy serene Prague.

You can feel the whole Prague by yourself.

Some photographers, who worked on the famous Charles Bridge, looked quite leisurely, except for a few. But please do not run too much.

I ran on a road paved with big stones, and later I could hardly walk well because my feet were throbbing with pain.

The reason I ended up spending 10 days in Czech was because of that Korean book. After finishing *Don Quixote and Brida. I couldn't find any new books written in Korean. So, I decided to find a book in Korean.*

I visited a Korean restaurant and asked the owner if I could buy a Korean book to read if it is finished but he gave me two books to encourage me.

I sat on a couch in the hostel and ended up reading all of the book, not noticing the passing of time.

Maybe I could feel a Korean feeling by reading the book which made me finish reading so fast.

While I was in Prague, Southampton's Europa League England team came to Prague to play. For sure, avid football fans from England also came to Prague.

Fans sat down at a restaurant in Prague's Old Town and sang, cheering songs for relays. There were as many people as any other famous tourist attraction in Prague for this time.

The Czech beer, much cheaper than England's and fabulous, might cause them to be excited and enjoy the moment.

As I was looking at them, I imagined getting to work in a team filled with players and supporters who are crazy for football and passionate about it.

I really wanted to channel all my passion into that kind of team.

How great is the synergy that passion and a positive mind would make? The synergy may create a miracle.

Bike Tour Tips in Czech Republic

Be Careful for Running

When I entered a famous city, I relaxed for a few days and ran in the morning or in the evening looking around the city.

But you need to be careful in this country.

Roads of other cities were also paved with stones like Prague's.

But, in Prague, the protrusion of the stones was worse compared to other cities.

One time, while running, the pain in the sole of my left foot was too severe to walk, or even straighten my foot enough.

Do Not Go Too Far into Nature

When riding in Czech Republic, which has wonderful natural scenery, I got onto the side road to see the beautiful nature and also to avoid cars.

If it's sunlight outside, there is no problem, but after sunset, it is so dangerous.

How Have You Been? Germany

Feeling Like Hometown, Nuremberg

Nuremberg is like the hometown in Germany that I visited again after a year and a half. The way of entering Nuremberg is so familiar to me.

It was the road where I always ran when I lived in Germany.

Along the path, I walked to the house where I had stayed without any intention.

Actually, I did not contact my old roommate, Chris, to let him know so I wanted to stop by it and see my old house at the outside.

But Chris, who was cleaning the kitchen window, saw me and yelled at me, "June," letting me in. "Wow, June! How could you be here?"

He said it was amazing.

I was standing there without any notice, like suddenly appearing from somewhere. Having been in Germany, I remembered to talk about my riding trip to Chris.

At that time, it was just a vague plan without thinking that I was really going to do it. Likewise, Chris said that when hearing my words, he thought 'His plan was weird.'" But I suddenly appeared making the abstract, joke-like plan true.

Chris and Lina gave a spare key for me to stay in and use whatever I needed. I felt grateful to have such a kind friend.

I wanted to stay more but had to leave for another plan to meet another friend, Malte. I met Malte while playing futsal on weekends in Germany.

He was one of my friends who got closer through football.

I had told him about my riding trip and he told me if I came to Germany by riding, he would join me.

But as I came to him on a bike, he said that this was crazy and he could not do it.

Anyway, the promise that we would ride together in Germany was not completed but he allowed me to stay in his house.

He lived with his girl-friends and got to be vegan too. Exactly one year ago, we played together having a barbeque party in a park, and it was hard to see him who changed a lot.

Malte and Chris did not have meat and it seemed to be a trend among young Germans lately. It was starting to change, said Linda, with a documentary about meat on TV.

Then, as more and more young Germans got vegans, who eats German sausage and who makes it? Speaking of Germany, it's about sausage, but will it not be made anymore? Luckily, they didn't stop to have a beer.

I also visited the dental lab where I had worked as an intern. For a surprise.

Petra, the receptionist of the lab, did not seem surprised but Stefan and Yaro, the manager, were so surprised to see me.

They were told that I had come from Korea by riding and they seemed to be very excited about it. Stefan served me lunch and took me to a shopping centre to buy warm clothes.

He bought me a beanie and hiking boots, saying that they were gifts from him and the other staff, and thanked me so much for coming to meet them without forgetting them.

Also, he said that I wish I could make my dream come true.

Whenever I got this kind of support, I felt some responsibility that I should make my dream come true.

Because if my dream comes true, I know that they will celebrate more than anyone.

Nuremberg is famous for the largest and oldest Christmas market in Europe.

This is one of the reasons that many tourists visit here in winter.

At the market, you are able to try the Nuremberg ginger cookie, which is really famous in Germany.

In Germany, it is a kind of culture to give ginger cookies as a Christmas gift and among them, the one from Nuremberg which has a long history is considered best preferred.

I recommend visiting the market at night instead of at noon.

There are more things not only to eat, but also to see and enjoy.

In the cathedral, a separate space was set up to have performances appropriate to the Christmas atmosphere, and there was also another place where you can learn about how other countries spend Christmas, and what foods they make for Christmas.

I visited Neuschwanstein Castle in Füssen during the period I stayed in Kaufbeuren for two days. It's about 50 kilometres which could be a full one-day course.

Luckily, the riding road was very well maintained.

I packed my bag with water, some snacks, a board for taking photos and headed to Füssen.

There were two other castles except the Neuschwanstein Castle.

One is Hohenschwangau Castle near Neuschwanstein Castle, and the other is HoHas Castle that is located in the old town.

Each castle has a unique atmosphere, figure and colour.

Neuschwanstein Castle has a steep spire, whose colour is white that is so and is very famous. It was made after the figure of Disneyland.

Hohenschwangau Castle is yellow and square-shaped, and it has a feminine feel, not a solemn one because of the colour.

The last one, HoHas Castle is red which makes it outstanding.

The first and second castle were the places where high-ranking people like kings and queens lived but the final castle located in the old town looked like a normal castle for local monarchs.

On the way to Füssen, I slipped and fell, going downhill and got into my first accident, which seriously injured me.

I went out early in the morning and the road was slightly iced due to the frost.

I took my luggage off the bike since I didn't need all that stuff for a long journey. I packed only for a one-day trip, which made the rear wheel too light and caused it to slip. I tried to ride cautiously, but unfortunately, an accident still occurred.

As I turned the steering wheel to the right at the end of the downhill, the front wheel turned to the right, the rear wheel didn't turn. I slipped on the floor, hit the wall of a building, banged my head twice on the ground and then curled up and lost consciousness for a few seconds.

When I woke up, the host of the house asked me if I was okay.

The clothes from the shoulders and thighs were torn, and there was some blood. Luckily, I wore thick clothes because it was winter so I didn't get serious injuries.

I decided to be careful when riding in the early morning.

Destiny to Meet Again

I had to go to the Netherlands but intentionally went to come down to the southernmost area of Germany.

It took more time and money but there was a reason why I did. It was in Mongolia.

I met a group of travellers who had a camping car in the morning. I kept running and saw a woman who waved her hand toward me.

I approached her to check if she needed some help.

It turned out that she did that to encourage me, who travelled by bicycle.

It was the time when I met a couple named Musch for the first time. They were travelling through Eurasia to participate in a programme made by a campervan travel agency.

They had a schedule from southern Germany, going through the Czech Republic, Poland, and the Baltic countries to Russia, Mongolia, and China, and then back to Europe on the Silk Road from China.

They invited me to stay in their house if I got to Germany. That was the first invitation that I got on the road and.

I could not refuse an invitation that I got for the first time. I must visit it! This was the reason why I moved to the southernmost area of Germany.

I met the Muschs in Mongolia, which was 2,843 kilometres, and met them again in Germany which was 15,213 kilometres from the beginning of the journey where I moved another 12,370 kilometres.

Their house was on a hill.

The first floor was where their sons lived and there was a living room and a kitchen on the second floor, and on the third floor there were rooms for the couple and their daughter.

The view of the Alps from the living room window on the second floor was so amazing. It was a beautiful house where I could see amazing landscapes out the window.

While staying there, I did trek in the Alps but also spent all the time eating and eating.

I woke up late and ate traditional food of Stuttgart made by the male host, apple pie made by the female host for snacks and I made tuna fried rice for dinner.

When I didn't cook, I sat on the couch and chilled out, staring at the Alps and reading books. It was so cosy like my home, and I even thought it would be a real my home.

　While riding a bicycle, meeting and talking with many people, I was learning many things by experiencing myself that I could not learn at school or in books.

I also learned a lot from other Warm Showers hosts Gitti and Martin, who invited me around Lake Constance.

In Particular, Martin, Gitti's husband, impressed me very much. He also travelled by bicycle.

He was a professor in a college and had a car that was over 30 years old, but he did not need a new car because he commuted by bicycle.

He had been doing a much better job than teaching students; that was finding abandoned and useless bicycles, repairing them in his underground workplace, and donating them to refugees for free. And then if they broke again, he repaired them again.

He said that he had started this thinking that if he presented bicycles to refugees, they could save the money for transportation.

When he cooked dinner, someone rang the doorbell and Martin guessed that it would be a refugee child.

When I heard what he was saying, I thought that it would be a joke. But when we went out, two refugee children were there.

Mrs. Gitti introduced them to me and said that they had a guest today and let them go.

Indeed, they often invited children from refugees to their house to help with their assignments, teach German, and give some allowance to them.

I heard a lot on the news about Europe struggling with refugees.

I saw the refugee children and the people who were willing to help them right before me and it was so touching and swelling.

Another peculiarity of the couple was that their children all lived out on their own and they got married over 50.

I heard that many Europeans live together without marriage and there would be many pros and cons.

I met the couple who had lived together for more than 30 years. The advantages and disadvantages depend on what people do and love.

I could indirectly feel that people could live together for a long time if they concentrated on strengths without making disadvantages.

Before I left their house, I wanted to say to Martin 'You are always right.'

As it was near Christmas, it was getting harder and harder to find Warm Showers hosts.

Christmas is a big holiday in Europe, so Europeans visit their hometown and spend Christmas with their family and friends.

If I visited Warm Showers host's house and spent Christmas together, it would be like having the whole family get together on New Year's Day or Chuseok, (the biggest holidays in Korea) with a foreigner guest.

So I made a plan to stay in a hostel at Freiburg for the Christmas holiday, but the night before the start of the Christmas break, I was matched with a Warm Showers host in the rural village of Horheim and could spend one night there.

The host, Alex, was an English teacher who was 2 years older than me and he told me that he would go to his hometown for Christmas. He suggested that I could stay at his house if I didn't find any accommodation during Christmas.

So I was able to find a place to spend Christmas for free.

Although he was an English teacher, had never travelled to a native English-speaking country such as England or the United States.

As he lived in Germany and learned English in his university, he could have a chance to stay in the UK. He had a plan to go to the UK for English training next summer and said that made him excited.

He was so nice.

He played the guitar well, had lots of fun and never talked without making a joke. football lover. He was a Bayern Munich fan.

To watch the Bayern Munich game, we went to a friend's house because she had a big TV and channels to watch football games with a one-year subscription, which made viewers comfortable.

Actually, her ex-boyfriend loved sports so they signed a one-year subscription but they broke up a few weeks ago.

Alex said it was good news for us because by taking bottles of beer and visiting her house, we could watch football games.

You'd be surprised to know how many hours Alex worked.

This is something that would never happen in Korea. He went to work only on Tuesdays, Thursdays, and Fridays when there were classes, and on Thursdays, he went to work at 10 o'clock as the first class was at 11 o'clock. I was jealous, but on the other hand, I had always been busy working, as growing up in Korea, people would spend lots of time working, so it was so strange to me and I wondered how this could be possible.

I stayed at Robert's house in Frankfurt on New Year's Day.

I met Robert at a hostel in Beijing, China and he invited me, who was travelling by bicycle in Germany to his house.

His parents went on vacation to Norway and during that time, he invited his friends to a New Year's party. Luckily, I stayed in his house during that period so I was able to experience the party with German friends.

I used to think that I would like to be invited to such a party; like a birthday party or a New Year's party which was held in a foreign house and it actually became a reality in Frankfurt.

We prepared snacks, beverages, beers and other types of alcohol, ready to meet 2017.

We decorated the living room with balloons and Robert, the host of the house, made dinner for people who came to the party.

It was just like what I had watched in movies. Loud music, playing games, drinking beers.

Before moving on to January 1st, we went to a bus stop with fireworks we had prepared, and set them off to welcome the new year.

A few weeks ago, there had been a terror attack at the Christmas Market at Berlin, so the New Year's fireworks festival in big cities in Germany was prohibited, and restraints against another terrorist attack could be seen.

But when I saw their fireworks, it was so messy, just like terror happened. Nevertheless, they kept enjoying the time throwing the fireworks on the road. They went crazy to play and I loved their style.

The next day, we went to the place where we had done the fireworks to take out some trash and cleaned up his house all together.

I thought this was what Germany was.

The last day of 2016 was already coming and it was time to meet January 1, 2017. It also meant that it had been half a year since I had started the trip.

Over the past half year, I met lots of people, communicated with them and learned what world they had lived in.

I was curious about how the world's other countries lived and if the cultures of Korea and their countries were same or different, or whether they had similar concerns and issues that I had faced growing up.

Many people whom I met for the trips were worried about food, clothing and shelter and were not satisfied with the society and establishment like me.

Also, they lived reflecting on their own situations.

They seemed to live their lives by finding a way to live happily, within the limitations of what they could do, no more or less.

Bike Tour Tips in Germany

Thermos

The hardest thing about riding to Germany was that I could not drink water even if I was so thirsty. The water I had brought was frozen or too cold to drink.

So, I used to melt candy in my mouth to choke on.

Warm Showers host gave me an unused thermos bottle and the problem was solved.

When it's cold, be sure to bring a small thermos. A sip of warm water quickly melts your body.

Morning Riding

In Warsaw, Poland, the snow clouds were out, but the cold stayed. The weather was heading to the top of winter.

In the morning, the frost on the bicycle path was frozen. It was much more slippery than I expected.

If you don't ride carefully, you would slip.

Evening Coming Soon

The sun rises for 9 hours only.

Compared to the time when I rode in Russia for 12 hours a day, the days were really short.

As a result, the distance I rode the bicycle should be reduced, and I had to leave early in the morning to arrive at my accommodation before the sunrise.

I think 100 kilometres seemed to be the most suitable distance.

Rhine River

Winter was coming and it snowed in Germany.

There were snow clouds for about a day in Germany but I could avoid the snow clouds by just riding along the Rhine River.

It's said that the temperature around the Rhine River is warmer compared to other places, thanks to the water temperature not dropping below 0 degrees, which creates a warmer environment.

Riding along the Rhine, I had been hit by rain but not by snow.

The Last Country on the Eurasian Continent, the Netherlands

Country of Bike

The unique thing that I saw in the Netherlands was bicycles.

The bicycle path was really well paved and so many people used bicycles.

It was strange for me to wait at the traffic light with other people on bicycles because I had never done that.

Especially in the morning rush hour, people including students and workers of all ages rode a bicycle to their destinations, so the bicycle paths were so crowded with them.

I was really shocked when passing Eindhoven Central station in the morning. There were so many bicycles that I doubted what I saw.

People who didn't find a place to park their bicycles, or who seemed a little bit late, just let their bike down and went to the train.

I wondered if they could find their own bicycle among so many bicycles. Also, I thought that it might be true that there were more bicycles than people.

I found one thing strange in the Netherlands where so many people used bicycles.

I needed to move from Roermond, the first city in the Netherlands to Eindhoven, which was 58 kilometres away.

When I was in Germany, they made a sign which showed the direction and place name of the place for that distance, but there was no sign in the Netherlands.

It was near Germany but had a completely different bicycle path system.

After wandering for a long time, I questioned passers-by for directions. As I asked one person on a bicycle how to go to Eindhoven, everyone around looked at me strangely.

"'You cannot get to Eindhoven by riding because it is too far from here. You should go to the train station and load yours.'"

I had ridden 100 kilometres a day, so when I heard the saying of loading my bicycle on a train to get there, it made me feel unsatisfied.

Because, I thought that so many Dutch who rode bicycles on the road so often would be willing to move 50 kilometres by riding. However, they asked me to move by train which made me feel nonsense.

I gave up using the bicycle path but rode by car to Eindhoven.

Once you visit the Netherlands, you should visit snack bars that can be easily found in the neighbourhood. As entering one of them, I felt like I was entering a Korean snack bar.

There were also some kinds of food that I could see in Korean snack bars.

The fried potato was not special, but the sauce was very special, including five sorts of them; ketchup, mayonnaise, mustard, peanut butter, and sour cream sauce.

Among them, I got recommended peanut butter. It was not too dry, a little sweet and had a fresh, like apple flavour.

A fantastic combination with fried chips. It would be high in calories but so good.

Once thinking about the Netherlands, the first thing that comes to mind would be tulips and windmills. It is clear that in the windy Netherlands, windmills are good movie power for the climate.

There was always at least one windmill in either cities or countryside, and the closer I got to the beach, the more windmills I could see.

It was a good chance to look at the inside of the windmill, and there were large and small wooden cogs meshing well with each other and rotating like one.

The wind power was used to move a large mortar to grind wheat into flour, and the smell of warm, freshly ground flour mixed with the smell of old wood filled the inside of the windmill.

I visited PSV and Feyenoord training centre in the Netherlands.

I happened to pass by to look around the PSV training centre and lounge, where everyone from youth to the adult 1 team worked out at the same place.

There was no 1st team on the training centre that day and only youth training. I thought that it was the best training centre which I had ever seen.

I felt that if I could work in this place, I would be really happy.

Meeting the Kuyt, the Symbol of Devotion

I visited another club, Feyenoord Training Centre, to meet a player named Kuyt, who had played for Liverpool when I was a student.

I remember him as a player who was sincere and dedicated to his team so I really wanted to meet him.

Feyenoord players took a minibus to enter the training ground and practiced.

On the first day when I visited the ground, I didn't know which entrance the minibus entered from, so I couldn't see the players enter the training ground and just saw them coming out after training. On the second day, I got to know the entrance and decided to let them notice me more actively, so I hung the Liverpool flag on my bicycle for them to look at me and stood holding a board with "KUYT" written on it, but my plan didn't work.

I went again the next day.

I put the same flag on my bicycle in the same place and waited, with the hanging white board. The first minibus carrying the players passed before me after getting signals.

The players on the minibus might have noticed me, who had been visiting for the three days, as they punched the window of the bus and opened the window to whistle.

When the second bus followed, they cheered me up much more.

The football players and the football coaches whom I had wanted to be when I was a child now cheered on me and I was really touched and moved.

It was hard to explain the emotion.

After their training, I was able to meet Kuyt, talk to him and take a picture.

We took pictures in Polaroid together and he wrote my name on the back of it. *Would he remember me if we meet again* someday?

I stayed the 90 days that I could stay in on the Schengen, and went on board from Rotterdam to Ipswich. I would finally enter the last country.

When I wake up tomorrow morning, I would hear the greeting "Good morning," right?

Bike Tour Tips in Netherlands

Learning a New Map

The Netherlands has bicycle paths in very good conditions like Germany. But it is a different bicycle path system from Germany.

In Germany, nearby cities are written on signs, but in the Netherlands, the number of bicycle paths are written on signs.

Following the bicycle path, you would find maps which are not quite helpful, so I recommend you to follow the mobile phone map apps.

Bicycle Traffic Jam

There is a joke saying the number of bicycles in the Netherlands is more than the population. I don't think it's a joke from my experience.

There are a lot of bicycles coming and going on the bicycle path.

Especially during rush hours, the number of bicycles increases so sharply.

Because there are so many bicycles on the narrow path, the traffic rules must be observed. You should not overtake and over speeding is so dangerous.

How to Protect Bicycles

It is said that there are as many bicycle robbers as the number of bicycles.

In the evening, the thieves took their trucks to take unlocked bicycles on the roads. So, keep your bicycle locked wherever you go.

This is similar to what the people of the countries said whenever I went through 10 countries. They told me the people in their countries are bad and steal bicycles, and warned me to lock it.

I, who travelled alone, always used to enter a supermarket without a lock on my bicycle, even though mine is at a greater risk of being stolen than others.

But nobody stole my bicycle.

I think it seemed too heavy to steal.

My Travel Destination, England

Good Morning – Welcome to UK

I finally got to England. The big difference was that I had to ride on the left. There were not many traffic lights and there were a lot of roundabouts. When going around the roundabout, I should turn clockwise. Another thing is language. Before entering the UK, I boldly spoke English without worries of mistakes. Because English was not only my mother tongue but also the people, whom I met. Now I am in England where they use English as their mother language and speak fluently and much faster.

It was fine for everyone to speak English wherever I went but when the conversation got more, I got a little intimidated.

It was totally fine to converse for small talk or normal life necessary communication in English. But I always avoided deep communication.

I arrived at Ipswich at 6 am. When I got off the ship, the weather forecast said it was five degrees below zero. The atmosphere at dawn was really cold. Fortunately I found my first warm shower host's house in the UK. It was in a small town named Maldon, where it took 80 kilometres away from Ipswich.

My first impression of England was cold. I wanted to ride when the sun rose and the temperature rose more but I couldn't find a good place to wait for. So I cycled as fast as I could to Colchester, the nearby city. I went to a cafe to make me warm and drink a cup of hot beverage. The downtown street was busy with students and workers heading to their workplace. I was alone who spent a long time in the cafe. Around 9 am I left Colchester to Maldon.

I contacted the host (Stephanie) to say that I arrived in Maldon. Stephanie relied me that she was absent but I could get in the house through the back door. I couldn't have entered the house when the owner was not at home, also I wouldn't go. Here is UK, where manners are really important. So I followed the road from the host's house, there was a dock, where seven boats were anchored. Sitting on a bench and enjoying the countryside of the UK, I waited for the host's message. I got a message that the host had arrived home and tried to take my bicycle to the hill and suddenly felt the pain on my right knee again. It hurt from time to time when I cycled in Europe, so I bought the keen band. The keen bank was working but this time is different as not as the previous pain. Stephanie, the host, made a reservation at a hospital so I could get treatment and massage at the hospital. The doctor advised me to finish my journey as soon as possible and take a rest. Before entering England, I made a cycling route. It is supposed to cycle along the English coastline and visit the football training grounds. I already searched all the training centres from the 1st to 4th leagues. Unfortunately I had to finish my journey as soon as possible because of my knees.

I made a new plan to Liverpool on the shortest route. I was not disappointed. My new route was not cycling the busy downtown of London, otherwise through North London, Oxford, Warwick, Stoke-on-Trent, and Chester to Liverpool.

From North London to Oxford, I rode along the side road by the canal and it was off-road where there were few cars and people. Of course it was nice for cycling in silence. I could see new landscapes. There were long boats anchored in the canal that apparently were just normal boats. But people are living inside of the long boats. The boats had a living room, at least two rooms, restroom and a kitchen. My friends explained to me that there were lots of houseboats on the Thames in London. The reason why people live there is that the houseboat is cheaper than the price of a house, especially in London.

The host of Warmshower at Oxford was a student at Oxford University and the other flatmates were also students of Oxford University. I admired people who are studying or have graduated from high-class university such as Seoul National University, Harvard University, and Oxford University. I thought that they are a different kind of people from me and they are living in their own league. That I couldn't interact in their class. But when I stayed at the house of the host who studied in Oxford, my stereotype totally disappeared. We hang out together doing indoor rock climbing and watching jazz concerts in a small pub. I played, drank, and enjoyed together with the people who I had admired before. As a human being without the background like education level, it is possible to make friends. I thought I had used to build walls in making relationships by myself. People don't make their friends at the level of school where the others graduated from. As I admired them, they envied my bicycle journey.

The routes to Liverpool would be made by the place where the warmshower hosts were matched. Warwick was one of the cities that I visited. There was a park with green grass and trees standing at the entrance to the city. As I crossed the river through the park, I saw a solemn castle looking down the city from the hilltop. Warwick was a small town but I could feel the nostalgia of the old city. Warwick has some things to see and there were many roads to take a walk which I liked. My host is a professional engineer working for a Jaguar. He worked for 7 years and now is planning to quit his job and to go to Bristol to farm. Farming would be definitely harder to work and make less income than working at the current company, but I respect his value and decision of growing good crops.

I got close to my final destination, Liverpool, Melwood. I sometimes worried that I might cry when I got to Melwood, but I am still on the way. It not was really over. I wanted to take pictures when arriving at Melwood during the day, not in the afternoon. Therefore I planned to stay in Chester, a city near Liverpool. Luckily, I could find the Warmshower's host there. The name of the host was Simon. Retiring from his work, he used to write some articles about the small issues in his city and send them to local newspaper companies or radios. His hobby is traveling by bicycle with his wife. While we were having dinner, he asked me how I had started this long journey. I answered these kinds of questions as I always did. Can you imagine how many times I got the same question on the road? So I had a repertory to answer and did that. 'I was not a football player, had no experience teaching football and just started this journey to become a football coach meeting several directors or coaches to get advice. My final destination is Liverpool because Liverpool FC is my favourite team.

Simon got interested in what I told and suggested a brief interview after dinner. The questions of the interview were quite basic. Age, where I come from, how long I took for the bicycle journey, and how many countries I travelled.

Finally, it was the day I enter Liverpool.

There was the River Mersey between Chester and Liverpool and I had to get on a boat to cross it. Simon said that it was a long tradition to take the boat to cross from Chester to Liverpool. Once I was arriving at the Liverpool dock I just remembered the time when I had been in Liverpool for a week on a backpacking trip. I slightly remember the way to Melwood. I followed my old memories. It was correct. There is Anfield stadium on the way to Melwood. I stopped by Anfield to take a picture and ride to Melwood. I finally arrived at the destination of my journey. I took pictures in front of the Liverpool logo at the entrance. Holding the Korean flag and arranging all luggage that I had carried for my journey.

Finish! Now I can take a rest! It did come the overwhelmed feeling or getting emotional. The rest was the majority of my head. On my way to a hostel I stopped by the supermarket to buy a sandwich for lunch. Once I bit the sandwich, spontaneously rang my phone bell. I took my phone and hear that "Here is BBC Northwest ~~~". Oh my… Now I remember that I gave my number to Simon. They were interested in the article that Simon had contributed to 'Northwest BBC' and contacted me.

After I was on the BBC, I received many greeting messages from my warmshower hostess. That was a much more emotional moment than ever!

Bike Tour Tips in England

Drive Left

Britain is the representative country that drives on the left side. When riding on the right road in other countries, I turned my head to the left to check if cars were coming or not, but when riding on the left, I had to turn my head to the right to Check. It was awkward at first but I was getting used to it. There were more rotaries than traffic lights. When passing rotaries, people should direct the direction with their hands and let the drivers who entered before the first pass after that.

Canals

There were so many canals connecting the cities and towns. When you want to ride enjoying nature, I recommend you to get on the canal. The landscape was good but the roads were not in good condition. It rained a lot with gloomy and cloudy days in the winter of the UK as everyone knows. The side roads of canals were not paved but dirt roads. The air was dry, maybe it is because of the weather and the soil got mud which made my bicycle vintage style. When taking a rest, I should get rid of the mud attached to the wheels. When the bicycle got too dirty, I took it to the canals to wash.

Paper Map

As it gets colder, the battery of the smartphone quickly goes out. Especially, when I put the phone on the cradle, the battery ran out quickly in a few hours and I could not use the maps on the phone. My idea was writing all the names of the cities and villages where I had passed on it. It was quite helpful and comfortable.

Epilogue

The long trip taught me two things. The first is the protection of the environment so that the beautiful natural scenery I have seen and enjoyed can be preserved so that others can enjoy it. Secondly, my journey would not have been completed if the precious help received during the long journey had disappeared. It is said that the aid received must be returned.

After the book was published in Korea, the entire sales cost of the book was donated to NGO Green Asia. During my trip to Mongolia, I met them and was indebted to them, and it was perfect for my taste because it was a group that planted trees in Mongolia to prevent desertification. As this English version was published, I wondered how the help I received would be returned.

When my trip to Liverpool ended and I was on BBC radio, the radio host asked me why my bike trip started. I had a similar saying: 'This journey started because I wanted to be a football coach.' I'm going to talk a little bit about my dream, which was also mentioned in the prologue.

I was born in a small city called Suncheon. I started to like football when I was young due to the influence of my brothers and relatives in my neighbourhood. Thanks to my fast running and physical strength, I enjoyed playing football with my friends. I kicked the ball as I ran around happily whenever there was a ball. Of course, my dream of becoming a football player grew, and I even went for a joining test at a local high school without my parents knowing it. My parents opposed my dream of becoming a football player. I could understand my parents' thoughts even at a young age and even now. At that time, the youth football system in Korea wasn't very good. If I said I wanted to grow into a football player around me, the first question to come back was whether I have a lot of money. I could also understand that my parents opposed it because the financial situation wasn't good at that time.

After that, my school days were not much different from those of my peers, and I went to the Department of Dental Technology. In the first semester of my third year, I stayed in Germany because I had the opportunity to be an intern at a dental clinic. By the time I was about to graduate, I began to wonder if my career should be fostered by the dental work. Even after the dream of becoming a football player of my school days came to an end, my dream of becoming a tactical assistant coach was kept in a corner of my mind. The dream began to wriggle again in Germany. I was convinced that it would increase the value of life to do what I want to do rather than to be highly paid and continue to work no matter how good the environment is.

I asked myself where and how it would begin. I thought that starting in Korea, where there is no money and no personal connections, and starting in Europe would not be much different. Then it occurred to me that if I started my career in Europe, where it is settled as a culture, I would not only learn football but also learn culture. The following questions were asked:" How? How should I begin?" The answer to these questions did not come out so easily. I only had an abstract desire to find the starting point, the bottom, and at the same time to learn under a good coach. But I couldn't build a realistic plan.

As the point of graduation approached, I started thinking that if I rode my bike to Europe, the home of football, and visited the training ground and shouted, "I want to learn football and I came here with this passion!" someone would reach out and help me.

After 6 months, I got on the bike.

Even on the burning asphalt in the Gobi Desert in Mongolia, and evcn in Siberia, where my hands and feet were freezing cold, I always said in my head, "It's Europe, let's hang on a little longer." I thought, if I arrived only in Europe, and when I arrived at the training ground, "My dream will come true as if the door of heaven opens." I was able to get to Europe by holding out like that, and I went around a lot of training grounds. The reaction was different from what I expected. Some of the coaches and players I met only sent me a message of support, "You can do it!" I realized after the trip was over the Liverpool International Academy to gain, and I am now gaining experience as a U18-year-old assistant coach at a local club named SV Olympiadorf in Munich and got a UEF. That I have to be qualified to learn from someone. In order to be like that, I need a certificate that must prove my qualifications. I finished my trip to Liverpool and was enrolled in the Football Coaching Admissions Course hosted by the Scottish Football Association. Over the past 5 years, I have gained experience at the Seoul National University football team and A C License in 2022.

Football led me all the way here. The road has never been smooth, and I find that the road to my dream, which is not yet over, is rough. Yet, it's believed that all these experiences have shaped me into the person I am today, Jungyu(June) Lee. It wasn't until I turned 30 that I realized how my career should be built up. As an adult who came back hard to make a dream about football come true and help children who are not given a chance even if they want to play football because of the poor system. Helping the children's dreams continue to grow. Helping to take less a roundabout way than me and helping to not walk the road hard. I think that is one of the ways in which the help I was given is returned in my own way.

Half of the loyalty will be donated to the Liverpool FC Foundation annually.

Acknowledgements

I learned a lot of things that I could not have learned at school while riding for 1,7190 kilometres in 235 days. I learned how to get closer to others, believe in them, live, love nature, get help from others, appreciate, challenge again, not giving up, most importantly, how to get encouraged and support each other. The people who cheered me and stopped their cars to shake my hand, cheered me with horns. It gave me the energy to keep riding.

I really want to express my gratitude to my parents, friends (YongJun, Lim Soomin, Sujong, GuSan) who always called and encouraged me. And lastly, I was really grateful to myself, who likes sports. I could get close easily to other people wherever I went.

Thanks to my translator Ji Eungin.

All the host of warmshower and couch-surfing, also other supporters;

Boris, Fan Zhang, Dashka Gere, Geraint Feuilly Schmidt, Bertek Mazur, Tobias Gyarfas, Simon Brown, Alexei

Email – *junkuy0319@gmail.com*
Instagram – June.gyu

obert Schmitz, Stefan Picha, Stepahnie Valentine,
er, Tatyaan, Dima Anoshin, Roman, Altras
gie), Margrita and Skol, Irene and Wolfgan
Malte von Rönne, Peter Reisner, Herha and Günter
obias Metz, Bärbel and Keit, Jerome Vidal, Ayur,
d Julen, Tanja, Anton, Gleb, Julia, Keth Kennard,
and the others.